AN INTRODUCTION TO
SHAKESPEARE

SCHOLASTIC BOOK SERVICES
New York Toronto London Auckland Sydney Tokyo

By the Same Author

Rhymes About the City
Rhymes About the Country
The Innocent Wayfaring
Geoffrey Chaucer of England
Shakespeare of London
The Search for God

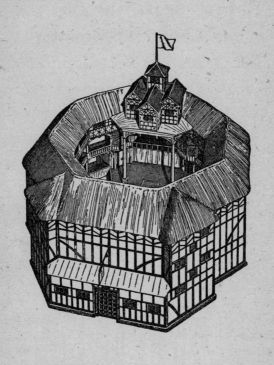

The MULTIPLE STAGE of the GLOBE PLAYHOUSE as reconstructed by John Cranford Adams

Irwin Smith

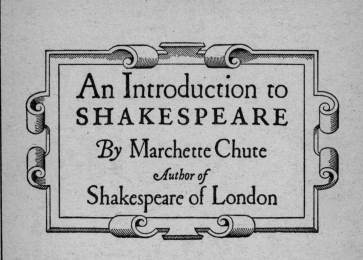

An Introduction to
SHAKESPEARE
By Marchette Chute
Author of
Shakespeare of London

E. P. Dutton and Company, Inc.
New York
Scholastic Book Services Edition

For M.G.

AN INTRODUCTION TO
SHAKESPEARE

Chapter 1

WHEN William Shakespeare was about four years old he had a chance to see his first play.

There had once been a yearly pageant in Stratford on St. George's Day, with a dragon that snorted fire made of real gunpowder. But the dragon had been put away six years before Shakespeare was born, and there had been very little makebelieve in Stratford until the day the actors arrived.

The acting company came on horseback, bringing a wagon for their costumes and their swords, their feathers and their drums. They went first to the mayor, to ask his permission to put on plays in Stratford, and the mayor for that year happened to be Mr. John Shakespeare, William's father. The mayor not only gave his permission but also arranged for a payment of nine shillings out of the town funds so that the first show could be seen by everyone without charge.

The actors put on their first show in the town hall, which was easy to change into a theatre. The main room was long and narrow, and a scaffold could be set up at one end of it with rows of benches below. At right angles to it was a smaller room, which the actors could use for changing their costumes. They had a great many costumes, because there were usually only six men in a company and the plays called for as many as twenty characters. An actor could change himself from a tinker to a Roman senator in as much time as it took him to slip out of a leather jerkin and into a colored robe, and he had a whole collection of beards to help his disguises. The beard was tied on with strings hidden under his hat, and if the actor was appearing in a bedroom scene and had no excuse for wearing a hat, the strings of his beard could be hidden under his nightcap.

The benches in the main hall filled quickly, since there was no way to reserve seats and everyone wanted to see the show. In Bristol once, when the actors gave a show at the town hall, so many people tried to get in that they broke the iron bar on the door. The children of Stratford could not expect seats of their own, since there was hardly room enough for the grown-ups, but they were allowed to stand between their fathers' legs where they could see and hear very well.

When a trumpet blew, everyone knew that the play was ready to begin. The actors could not dim the lights and raise a curtain, since they had no stage lights and no curtain on their raised wooden scaffold. Instead, a single actor strode onstage; and, since there were no printed programs, he announced to the audience what the play was going to be about.

This actor was called the Prologue and he looked very stately in his glittering robes. His speech was in rhyme, for verse was much more popular than prose on the Elizabethan stage. The actors liked it, because it was easy to memorize, and the audiences liked it because it was so musical. A small company of actors did not have room to carry many musical instruments, except drums and trumpets, and the strong, rhythmical effects that the audiences loved came to them mostly through the verse. It could hardly be called poetry, since the men who wrote the plays were not poets. But the rhymed speeches sounded very effective when some impressively bearded actor boomed them forth to the awed listeners on the benches below.

The audience expected more than poetry in their plays. They also expected violent, realistic action. In a play called *Horestes*, for instance, a savage battle takes place outside the city walls, and the playwright makes clear in his stage directions that he expected the actors to stage a real fight. "Go and make your lively battle and let it be long, ere you can win the city." Except for the battle itself, the scene onstage would not have looked very realistic, since the city walls were portable ones, put up in full view of the interested audience, and the ancient Greeks were dressed in ordinary Elizabethan doublets. But no one in the audience objected to this as long as the play was exciting.

The only kind of realism the audience wanted was in the action itself, and if the action called for a head to be cut off they expected to see it happen. In a play called *A New Tragical Comedy of Appius and Virginia*, the heroine's head is cut off in full view of the audience. This was done through sleight-of-hand, with a bladder of animal blood and a carved property head, and the actors had to be very clever to make the substitution with the small boys in the audience watching alertly from the front benches. On the other hand, the author of this same play wanted to convince the audience that Virginia's death would always be remembered, and so an actor named Memory comes onstage carrying a small, portable tomb. The audience had no difficulty in accepting a realistic beheading in the same play with a symbolical Memory, any more than they objected to the fact that Memory, although she was supposed to be a woman, was played by a man. The plays of Shakespeare's boyhood were an extraordinary mixture of violent action and jokes, of blood and trumpets and moral maxims, and the playwright put in anything whatever that he thought might be effective.

The moral maxims were an important part of the show, since if each play had not taught a lesson of some kind the careful parents of Stratford would not have wished their children to go to the theatre. The Elizabethans had moral maxims everywhere, even printed across their wall decorations and in the children's school books, and each play was expected to teach a lesson. For instance, a play called *The Cradle of Security* told about a king who spent his time frolicking with beautiful ladies named Pride and Luxury until at last he was turned into a pig. A small boy in Gloucester saw the play when he was about Shakespeare's age and was so excited by the transformation scene that when he was a grown man he could still remember the color of the actors' costumes and the fact that it took three wires to fasten the pig mask over the king's head.

The plays in England had once been church plays, shown in the streets of the towns to act out stories from the Bible, and it was discovered very early that a small devil made a good comic character. This little devil came to be called the Vice, and he turns up under various names in the plays of this period. In one he is called Ambidexter, in another Inclination, and in another he is called Haphazard, but in each case he is the same character, a lively mischief-maker who gets the other members of the cast into as many difficulties as he can. The playwright did not want the small boys in the audience to go home with the monkey-like pranks of the Vice running through their heads and so he would close the play with moral reflections uttered by a character like Virtuous Life or Good Fame. As for the Vice, he rode off to hell on Lucifer's back, and the audience knew that it was Lucifer, the Devil, because his name would be written on both the front and the back of his costume.

When the actors had finally packed up their properties and left Stratford, the small boys in town could act out the plays over again in the elm-shaded streets or down by the river Avon. A small French prince, no older than they were, saw a group of English actors perform at the French court and was so fascinated by a beheading scene that he went around for days afterwards pretending he was the whole company, since he had no one to play with and had to take all the parts himself. The children of Stratford could not have been any less excited by their first plunge into the world of makebelieve, and for many nights the clowns and the trumpets and the long rolling verses must have entered into their dreams.

Nearly every year after that the actors came back to Stratford. The town was visited both by local companies and by the great London actors who had played before Queen Elizabeth, and they brought with them all the latest plays. Every year the small boys of Stratford could watch them unpack their wagons, and some of them must have had visions of growing up to be actors themselves. But most of them became farmers or storekeepers, and the only boy in the group who finally became an actor was the son of the prominent glovemaker and former mayor, Mr. John Shakespeare.

Chapter 2

ALL OVER England the acting companies stopped their wagons and set up their stages. Sometimes they used town halls, like the one in Stratford, and sometimes large private houses, but usually they acted in the courtyards of the local inns. Every town had at least one inn—Stratford had four—and the actors found that they could build a scaffolding at one end of the innyard and have their penny audience stand in front of it, while the wealthier people leaned out of the upstairs windows and looked down on the stage below.

The actors used the London inns so often that they built permanent scaffoldings at a large inn like the Cross Keys; but even the best of them had disadvantages. It was not easy to collect the entrance money, with so many people coming and going, and there was no way to store the costumes and the properties. Moreover the actors had to share the innyards with the carters, who used them several times a week to pack their freight wagons and meet their customers.

What the actors needed was a theatre building, and when Shakespeare was twelve years old a Londoner named James Burbage decided to build one. Burbage was a prominent actor and in his youth he had been trained as a carpenter. To these advantages he added a single-minded, vigorous optimism and a great love of the theatre; and with the full support of his lively wife, he set out to build the first theatre in England.

Burbage raised the money by persuading his wife's brother that a theatre would be a better investment than the grocery business. But the two men quarreled steadily all the time the building was going up, partly because Burbage had such lavish ideas. He was determined to make his theatre the finest building in England, with the best oak timber and the most glorious painted decorations. The land on which he was building was out beyond Finsbury Fields and a long way for the average Londoner to walk, but Burbage was convinced that if he made his building large enough and fine enough it would be a success.

There was no theatre in England, or even in Europe, that Burbage could use as a model, so he had to work out his own design. He made it somewhat like the innyards, with a stage jutting into a courtyard and seats arranged in tiers overhead, and he planned to use the same system of charging a penny for standing room and more for the upstairs seats. But since he wanted everyone to see the stage easily he made the building round, like the great amphitheatres that were being used south of London for bear-baiting, and, like them, he made his building open to the sky. There was a ring of thatch around the outside to protect the seats and the actors' rooms, and there was also a slanting cover over the stage itself. James Burbage was an actor and he knew how much money had been invested in the velvets and satins of the theatre costumes.

If James Burbage had planned the wrong design he would have been ruined, and it would have been a long time before anyone else attempted to build a theatre in England. But Burbage knew his business, and the theatre was an instant success.

An Introduction to Shakespeare

"Thither run the people thick and threefold," said a Londoner, and what was called "the gorgeous playing place erected in the Fields" became as much a showplace for tourists as Westminster Abbey or the Zoo. Other London businessmen began to invest in theatres also and to put up large and handsome buildings like the Curtain, the Rose and the Swan. But these men were drapers or starch-makers and built the theatres only to make money. James Burbage remained the one real theatre man in the business, and he went on calling his building simply the Theatre.

The actors had many reasons to be grateful to Burbage. They no longer had to move out for the carters, and they had a large, contented audience safely installed before the show started. They had a storage place for their scripts and their piles of expensive costumes, as well as for their huge clutter of properties that included everything from gilt spears and cauldrons to portable castles and tombs, and they also had adequate dressing rooms for the first time in their strenuous lives.

Above all, they had the latest in stage equipment and design, for Burbage had given them five different levels on which to produce their plays. At the lowest level were the trapdoors, built into the floor of the stage, and an actor who was playing a devil could crouch on a little platform, be drawn up to the stage level, and leap out with an explosion of fireworks as realistically as though he had just come from the infernal regions. Ghosts could do the same; and if the actors needed a grave or a ditch they could pull the platform up halfway and leave it there, with perhaps a small plaster tree or a bank of imitation moss to show that the scene was taking place outdoors.

An Introduction to Shakespeare

The next level was the main stage and here the actors produced all their most important scenes. The jutting front area could be used for coronations and wars and city streets, and behind it was a small inner stage that could be used as a shop or a study. Above this, on the next level, was a balcony which could be used for anything from a mountain to a city wall. If a town was besieged in a play, for instance, the invaders gathered on the main stage and the besieged townsmen fought them off from the balcony.

Just under the roof of the Theatre, Burbage had installed a series of pulleys, so that if a play called for a goddess to be wafted down from the heavens she could be wafted down with great dignity. Up there, under the roof, a man could also send down thunderbolts, or stuffed birds, or warning hands clutching swords, and he could imitate the rattle of rain or anything else that was called for in the script. There was also room aloft for the musicians, ready with trumpets for the battle scenes or hautboys for coronations, although the musicians were moved about and sometimes even played from under the stage. Anything could be shown in the Theatre, from a storm at sea to the chariot of the sun, and every year the actors could work out new and astonishing stage effects for their audiences.

The more money the actors made, the more they could spend on their scripts. In the old days the actors got most of their scripts by paying sixpence in a London bookstall and buying a printed copy of a play. The title-page told at a glance how many actors were needed and how the parts could be divided up and sometimes even gave suggestions on the costuming. But the profits went to the bookstore rather than to the playwright, and there was very little incentive for a good poet to write plays.

All this was changed as the great new theatres began to go up in London. The acting companies constantly needed new scripts, since there were a great many seats to fill and a different show was presented every afternoon. They were willing to pay six or seven pounds for a play, but they expected it to be a practical theatre script and one that would really attract audiences.

Many young writers at the London law schools and the universities had been turning out plays, but they were not the kind that professional actors could use. The young men tried to obey a set of rules that they had been taught in school, and these rules did not interest the ordinary London audience. One rule said, for instance, that it was wrong to show a murder onstage; and so the famous play of *Gorboduc* has each of its many murders reported by messenger, with the rest of the time filled in by stately speeches in blank verse.

Gorboduc was written by two young men in the London law schools and produced for their own amusement. It was highly praised, even by the great Sir Philip Sidney, but it was not the kind of thing that professional actors could present to their regular audience. The Londoners liked "stately speeches and well-sounding phrases" just as much as Sidney did, but they did not consider them a substitute for action. If there were to be any murders they wanted them onstage, with real blood. Nor did they see any reason why a play should obey the classical theory of the unities and have all its action take place in a single location on a single day. They liked a play to roam about to far-off, romantic places like Venice or Babylon, and they did not object in the least if the hero was a young man in the first act and had grown-up children in the third. If the young writers who had been educated at the universities wanted to appeal to the Londoners they had to use a larger, looser, freer way of writing than the one that was taught at Oxford and Cambridge; and they soon learned it.

When Shakespeare was in his early twenties, the most popular play on the London stage was an Oriental melodrama called *Tamburlaine*. It had been written by a young university man named Christopher Marlowe and presented by a brilliant company of actors who gave the play all the glitter and violence and excitement that Marlowe had put into the writing. There were spectacular scenes, and the audience could see the captive kings dragging Tamburlaine's chariot or the governor of Babylon hanging in chains while real bullets flew around him. There were magnificent costumes, and beautiful resonant voices, and behind it all the great ground swell of the poetry. For Marlowe was a real poet, the first of his kind to write for the public theatres, and many a London apprentice must have walked out of the theatre into the late afternoon sun with the magic of the lines beating through his head.

There were many young writers like Marlowe who had been sent to the universities on scholarships or through the careful economy of their parents, and who found there was nothing to do with their expensive educations afterwards. They turned to the stage, and nearly every young poet of the period tried his hand at writing plays. The most successful financially was Robert Greene, who might have been a rich man if he had not spent his money as fast as he made it. Greene was a practical journalist and he gave his audiences whatever he thought they would like. He stuffed his plays with murders and fairies and devils and was a specialist in remarkable stage effects like Venus sailing upwards into the clouds or Jonah "cast out of the whale's belly upon the stage."

The most delicate sense of comedy belonged to George Peele, who parodied the ghosts that were so popular on the London stage and who also made fun of the long, hexameter line with which some of the English writers had been trying to experiment. According to Peele, it sounded like this: "Dub dub-a-dub, bounce, quoth the guns, with a sulphurous huff-snuff." Another lively wit was Thomas Nashe, who insulted his elders and betters in a series of pamphlets but is chiefly known for the lovely lyric he wrote for one of his plays:

> Brightness falls from the air,
> Queens have died young and fair . . .

Another popular writer was Thomas Lodge, who wrote plays by himself or in collaboration with Greene and who was convinced he was betraying his classical education by stooping to please the "penny-knaves" who flocked to the public theatres. The group as a whole has been called the university wits and the title would have pleased them, since they were proud of their education and felt superior to the actors who bought their work.

Robert Greene in particular was fond of pointing out that he had been educated at both universities and that actors were inferior beings who would be quite useless without him and his fellow playwrights. It therefore came as a special shock to him when one of the great successes of the theatre season of 1592 was written by a London actor who did not have a university education. The play was *Henry VI*, and the London actor was William Shakespeare.

An Introduction to Shakespeare

Greene was very ill in the autumn of 1592, and he had spent all his money. He felt that this was somehow the fault of his former employers, the actors, and he wrote a violent pamphlet in which he accused them of being apes and monsters. He implored his literary friends like Marlowe not to supply them with any more plays and he made a special attack on a single actor who, "with his tiger's heart wrapped in a player's hide, supposes he is as well able to bombast out a blank verse as the best of you; and being an absolute *Johannes fac totum*, is in his own conceit the only Shake-scene in a country." The phrase about the tiger's heart is a parody of a line in *Henry VI* —"O tiger's heart wrapped in a woman's hide!"—and the Latin phrase means that Shakespeare was a kind of Johnny Do-Everything. He was a successful actor, and now, according to Greene's bitter report, he felt he could be a successful playwright also.

Greene died before the pamphlet appeared and his publisher, Henry Chettle, crossed out some of the more violent passages before he printed it. He said later that he was sorry he had not crossed out the attack on Shakespeare also, since he had heard that Shakespeare was a good writer and upright in his business dealings and knew by personal experience that he was a courteous man and an excellent actor.

Chettle was sympathetic to writers—he later became one himself—and it was characteristic of him to apologize to Shakespeare. But it was extremely fortunate that he published Greene's attack without altering it. If he had not, there would have been no way of knowing that in 1592 Shakespeare was already an established actor on the London stage.

Chapter 3

SHAKESPEARE was twenty-eight years old when Robert Greene attacked him as an actor who dared to write plays and Henry Chettle defended him as a good playwright and an excellent actor.

Most of Shakespeare's fellow actors had been trained in the profession since childhood but Shakespeare himself entered it comparatively late. When he was eighteen years old he was still in Stratford. And he had apparently intended to settle down there since in the autumn of his eighteenth year he married a woman named Anne Hathaway, who belonged to a well-to-do farming family in a nearby village. There were three children in the next two years, a daughter named Susanna and then twins named Hamnet and Judith.

Stratford was a rather rigid and conservative little town and many young men left it to go up to London. Richard Field, for instance, left Stratford when he was fifteen to become apprenticed to a London printer and within ten years he owned the business. But publishing was a respectable business, while most people were convinced that acting was not; and there must have been many citizens of Stratford who were sorry to see the eldest son of a respected man like John Shakespeare take up so shiftless and vagabond a career.

An Introduction to Shakespeare

Whatever an outsider might believe about the lazy life of an actor, the actors themselves knew what long hours of hard work and what strenuous years of preliminary training went into their profession. Audiences had become much more critical than they were in the old days when Shakespeare was a boy and the stages had become much larger and more elaborate. In the early days an actor could jump down from behind a piece of painted canvas and convince an audience that he had been thrown from a city wall, but now he took a fall from the balcony of the Theatre and had to be a trained acrobat to land realistically without damaging himself or his costume.

An actor also had to be a trained swordsman, for the London audiences knew a great deal about the art of fencing and the Theatre was often hired for exhibition matches by professionals. A good fencer needed years of training and a great deal of physical endurance, for the heavy Elizabethan rapier was a brutal weapon and the fencer was trained to make for his opponent's eyes or strike below the ribs. Actors had an even more difficult problem, since they had to face a critical audience on an open stage in the glare of the afternoon sun and stage a duel which was realistic enough so it would look as though a man had actually been killed.

The actors also had to be dancers, since it was the custom to end every play with some kind of dance and most of the playwrights introduced dances wherever they could into the play itself. London was full of excellent dancing schools, where a young man could learn to do spectacular leaps and swing his partner through the air, and when he had paid his penny to go to the Theatre he expected a much more remarkable performance from the professionals on the stage.

An Introduction to Shakespeare

It was also taken for granted that an actor should be able to play a musical instrument, and many of the greatest actors of London were still listed officially as musicians after years of appearing on the stage.

Most important of all, the actor had to have a good voice. The London theatres were very large and many of the seats were a long way from the stage. There were no programs and very little scenery, and it was therefore through the actors' voices that the audience learned the identity of the speakers and the location of the action. When Shakespeare was a boy the actors had done a good deal of strutting about and shouting, which matched well enough the "huffing" parts the playwrights had written for them. But by the time Shakespeare became an actor, poets like Christopher Marlowe were beginning to write beautiful and subtle poetry for the stage, and the actors were learning the brilliant, clear, rapid delivery that such plays required.

One problem that still remained from the old days was that of doubling, since an actor might still be required to fill several roles in a single afternoon. In one London production of this period an actor took eight parts, including a ghost, a nobleman, a child and a soldier, and this was not felt to be at all unusual. Doubling was not an easy system, especially since the play was a different one every afternoon, and an actor needed a vigorous body and a good memory to get through all his parts successfully.

An actor who could not meet the exacting requirements of the London theatre usually joined one of the provincial companies; or he went abroad to Germany or the Netherlands, where the audiences "flocked wonderfully" to see the English actors and the women fell in love with them. But the actors themselves wanted to be a success in the intense, competitive life of the London stage. Shakespeare belonged to this life and it is no wonder that Chettle said he was an "excellent" actor. He must have been, or he would not have remained for long in London.

It was not unusual for a London actor to try his hand at writing plays, since he knew so much at first hand about stage-craft and about the reactions of an audience. Richard Tarleton, the great comedian, wrote a very successful play, and another popular actor named Thomas Heywood estimated at the end of his long career that he had written all or part of more than two hundred plays. Shakespeare was only one of several actors who turned to play-writing, and what is chiefly noticeable in his case was his instant success with the public. Robert Greene would have felt no jealousy towards an unsuccessful writer and in any case the popularity of *Henry VI* is a matter of record. It was produced at the Rose on the third of March, 1592, and played to large and excited audiences all season.

Henry VI was written in three parts, so that it is really a series of three plays, and Shakespeare put into it everything he felt his audiences would like. He used all five levels of the stage, with the main stage for council rooms and city streets and even Westminster Abbey. He used the balconies to show the besieged town of Orleans, which the actors who played the English attacked with scaling-ladders from the stage, and he even used the turret on the top level for Joan of Arc to thrust out a flaming torch. He used the trapdoors also, and an actor dressed as a spirit rose up through a garden while the duchess watched from her balcony and the property man supplied thunder and lightning aloft. There were also stirring atrocity scenes, with plenty of blood, and four severed heads were brought onstage.

What really made the play popular, however, was its patriotic attitude towards English history. According to *Henry VI*, any Englishman was a match for ten Frenchmen and Joan of Arc defeated the gallant English only because she was assisted by magic. This was not history but the Elizabethans liked to think it was, and Tom Nashe reports that the whole audience was in tears during the scene in which Lord Talbot dies on a French battlefield holding his dead son in his arms.

Shakespeare knew how a man would feel about his dead son:

> Come, come, and lay him in his father's arms . . .

But he also knew that the audience at the Rose would expect a rhyming line to follow, and all he could think of was "harms." So he wrote:

> My spirit can no longer bear these harms.

This was not the sort of line that Shakespeare would have written five years later, but every writer does apprentice work at first. Moreover, Shakespeare was in a hurry. He was trying to compress an enormous amount of material from a history book called Holinshed's *Chronicles* into a manageable stage production, and he had time to work on the play only when he was not busy with his acting profession.

Another play he wrote at about the same time was *Titus Andronicus*, and this also was very popular, rivalling the success of a brilliant and bloody melodrama by Thomas Kyd called *The Spanish Tragedy*. Shakespeare's play is full of drums and processions and murders and burials, and there is much cutting off of heads and hands. None of this seems very tragic, since the people are not recognizable human beings, but the young playwright worked out some effective theatrical situations and the play had a long life on the London stage.

At about this same time Shakespeare also wrote a farce, which he called *The Comedy of Errors*. The joke revolves around two sets of twins who are mistaken for each other all through the play, and Shakespeare kept his complications moving smoothly and at top speed. Plays on this particular subject had been popular with Italian audiences for years and they were equally popular with the English. Endless complications could arise from a case of mistaken identity, with the audience enjoying the superior feeling of knowing more than anyone on the stage; and *The Comedy of Errors* had a long and prosperous career.

Shakespeare was a writer who needed room to experiment and he was willing to try anything. He sent his roots wide before he sent them deep, and he began his career as a playwright by doing many kinds of plays. He wrote a history play in *Henry VI*, a Roman tragedy in *Titus Andronicus*, an Italian farce in *The Comedy of Errors*, and then tried something entirely different and wrote a light English comedy in *Love's Labour's Lost*.

Love's Labour's Lost is a charming game with words, and it depends on an audience that is sufficiently interested in words to enjoy the joke. This particular fashion in writing had been started by a poet named John Lyly, who wrote plays for a small private theatre in which all the actors were children. Many people tried to use Lyly's style in their ordinary conversations, and the lords and ladies in *Love's Labour's Lost* talk the way many young people of London hoped they sounded but seldom did. The play is as light as a soap bubble, but it ends when the lords resolve to give up all fancy phrases in their love making and talk straight English.

Every comedy was expected to have a song, and Shakespeare wrote two for *Love's Labour's Lost*. The first is a spring song:

> When daisies pied and violets blue
> And lady-smocks all silver-white
> And cuckoo-buds of yellow hue
> Do paint the meadows with delight . . .

The second is a winter song:

> When icicles hang by the wall,
> And Dick the shepherd blows his nail,
> And Tom bears logs into the hall,
> And milk comes frozen home in pail . . .

There were many good poets writing for the English stage, Marlowe and Peele and Nashe and lesser writers who shared the wonderful Elizabethan gift of words and made it a lyric age. But the young playwright from Warwickshire who had appeared on the horizon was already showing signs of being a poet greater than any of them. Greene had good reason to be frightened by his approach, for Shakespeare might be a courteous man but he was already a formidable writer.

Chapter 4

IN 1592, when Shakespeare was just beginning his career as a playwright, the plague came to London. The mayor at once ordered the closing of the theatres and they remained closed for nearly two years, while the spiders wove cobwebs in the galleries and the actors toured the country villages. One group of actors lost so much money that they had to pawn their costumes and properties, and the two most important London companies had to combine forces in order to stay in existence.

Shakespeare could still find work as an actor, but as a playwright he had nothing to do. None of the companies could afford to buy new plays, and even the old ones had to be shortened for country audiences. So Shakespeare turned to another kind of writing and did a narrative poem instead.

The poem was called *Venus and Adonis* and it was handsomely printed by Richard Field, the young man from Stratford who had become a successful publisher in London. It was the custom in those days to dedicate every book to some prominent person, or even to several prominent people at once, and Shakespeare dedicated his to the Earl of Southampton. The Earl was nineteen years old and a very romantic figure with his satins and jewels. Many writers, from Shakespeare to

An Introduction to Shakespeare

Nashe, dedicated their work to him, and if he liked a poem he could be expected to make its author a handsome present.

The Earl of Southampton liked *Venus and Adonis*, and so did everyone else. It was even said that the young men at the universities slept with a copy of it under their pillows and kept a portrait of the author on their study walls. One of the chief publishers in London, John Harrison, took over the copyright from Field so that he could publish the poem himself, and it was so popular that it went through ten editions in Shakespeare's lifetime.

Venus and Adonis appealed to younger readers because it was a love story, but Shakespeare's next poem, *Lucrece*, was able "to please the wiser sort," as one elderly Elizabethan critic put it. This poem also was dedicated to Southampton and published by Harrison, so that it was launched under the patronage of two very important men, and it was warmly received by the reading public. *Lucrece* went through four editions in six years and was lavishly quoted in anthologies of the period.

Both poems were favorably received by the critics, and writer after writer expressed his admiration for them. As Richard Barnfield said, four years after *Lucrece* had been published, the two poems had put Shakespeare's name in "fame's immortal book"—a remark which no one had ever made about his plays.

Shakespeare now had a prominent businessman for his publisher, one of the greatest earls in England for his patron, and a reading public that was eagerly waiting to buy his next poem at the bookstalls. It should have been an intoxicating moment for the country boy in Warwickshire and he should have begun at once on another poem.

An Introduction to Shakespeare

But Shakespeare was not an ordinary writer, and he did not do what was expected of him.

The year *Lucrece* was published, Shakespeare stopped writing for publication entirely. Instead he joined a new acting company that had just been formed, and for the rest of his career he wrote plays for that company alone. He made no effort to get these plays published, and it was only through the devotion of two of his fellow actors, several years after his death, that the plays were finally collected for the reading public. In spite of his great success, he wrote no more narrative poems for Harrison and Southampton, and he became the only poet of the Elizabethan era who concentrated his attention on writing for the stage.*

Shakespeare did not care what the literary world thought of him. All he wanted was to be free to work in his own way. He would not have had this freedom if he had gone on trying to please Harrison and Southampton, since he would have been expected to write the kind of poetry—ornamental and lavish and correct—that was currently fashionable and to repeat his earlier successes instead of experimenting with something new.

The acting company which Shakespeare joined in 1594 gave him the freedom he wanted, as the great range and variety of his work from that time forward bear witness. No one but Shakespeare himself is responsible for the greatness of his plays. But the actors of his company gave him loyal, intelligent support and space in which to experiment, and the penny public of the ordinary London theatres gave him their de-

---

* The only non-dramatic poetry he wrote was a series of sonnets, which were passed about among his friends and then published, apparently without his consent, many years later.

An Introduction to Shakespeare

voted patronage. The literary men of London looked with contempt upon these "penny knaves," but the approval of the regular theatre public was good enough for Shakespeare.

We think of the company now as being "Shakespeare's company," but he did not think of it like that. Every actor in it had equal importance, and all of them were brilliant and successful men of the theatre. If anyone in the company could have been called a star when it was formed in 1594, it would have been Will Kempe, the most popular comic actor of his day and the successor of the great Tarleton himself. The theatre had come a long way since the days of Shakespeare's boyhood when the comedy figure of the Vice dominated so many of the plays, but the clown was still an important personage and Kempe was the greatest clown of his day.

When the new company made its first appearance at Court, three of its members collected the money: Shakespeare, Kempe and a third actor who later became the idol of all theatre-going London. This was Richard Burbage, son of the actor who had built the Theatre. Richard had his father's hot temper, and when James Burbage was once involved in one of his numerous fights, Richard seized a broomstick and sailed wholeheartedly into the fray, with his mother assisting. He inherited also his father's ardent love of the theatre and gave it thirty five years of devotion. He worked in extremely close association with Shakespeare, and it was Richard Burbage who first acted the parts of Hamlet and Othello and King Lear. He was fortunate in having Shakespeare to write such parts for him, but Shakespeare was fortunate also in having so brilliant an actor to interpret them. Like everyone else in that wonderful company, they benefited each other.

Another important member of the company was John

An Introduction to Shakespeare

Heminges. During the first years of its existence the company experimented with various paymasters (this was the post that Kempe, Burbage and Shakespeare shared the first year) but they eventually settled down with Heminges as their permanent business manager. Heminges protected their interests, conducted their lawsuits and even brought up some of their children; and he handled the enormous sums of money that the company earned with such efficiency that in one case all the London acting companies asked him to act as their agent. His closest neighbor was Henry Condell, another actor in the same company, and it was these two men who later brought out the first complete edition of Shakespeare's plays. They did it "without ambition either of self-profit or fame; only to keep the memory of so worthy a friend and fellow alive as was our Shakespeare," and many of Shakespeare's greatest plays would have been lost if it had not been for Heminges and Condell.

Even the people who hated the acting profession were obliged to admit that some actors were "honest householders and citizens well thought of among their neighbors." This is a good description of most of the men in Shakespeare's company, who were careful taxpayers and highly respected citizens. Heminges and Condell lived in a handsome residential district on the west side of town, where they were active in church work and brought up large families; Heminges had fourteen children and Condell had nine. On the other side of town Richard Burbage had a house near his father's theatre; he had seven children and when thieves broke into his house they made off with five little children's aprons. Most of the other actors in the company were family men also. Richard Cowley had four children, Augustine Phillips had five, and although Thomas Pope had no wife he adopted a whole succession of fatherless children and hired a housekeeper to look after them. Shakespeare himself had three children, but they were apparently brought up in Stratford and he spent most of his time in London in hired lodgings.

The new company was off to an excellent start in the spring of 1594, since the Lord Chamberlain himself was their patron. The chief difficulty was in finding a suitable theatre, since all the London theatres had been closed by two years of plague. The Chamberlain's company was finally obliged to rent a small and unsatisfactory theatre that stood south of London in the little village of Newington. They got it for ten days only and during that time were obliged to share it with their rivals, the Admiral's company.

Neither company had any new plays and both of them used their most reliable old ones. In the case of the Admiral's company this was *The Jew of Malta*, a bloody and improbable melodrama written by Christopher Marlowe. In the case of the Chamberlain's company this was *Titus Andronicus*, a bloody and improbable melodrama written by William Shakespeare. The latter was an exceptionally popular play and had been produced by three different London companies before it and its author settled down permanently with the Chamberlain's company.

Shakespeare's company still had found no theatre for themselves when the season opened in London that autumn, so they rented one of the London inns. This was the Cross Keys, which had the advantage of being much closer to the center of town than the Rose or the Theatre and which had been used by actors so often that the management had erected a permanent stage.

An Introduction to Shakespeare

The chief difficulty with the Cross Keys was the fact that the mayor of London was strongly opposed to allowing plays within the city walls, and it took the influence of the Lord Chamberlain himself before the mayor would give Shakespeare's company a license. It was finally agreed that the actors would open quietly and not advertise the play by marching through the streets with drums and trumpets as they did in the smaller towns. They would also give part of each day's receipts to the poor people of the parish, and they would start promptly at two o'clock in the afternoon so that the young people in the audience would be able to get home before dark.

The mayor of London strongly disapproved of young people going to plays and said so frequently. He would have kept them away altogether if he could, but in spite of his position and influence there was nothing he could do to stop them. Young Londoners were determined to go to plays, and they were particularly determined to go to the plays of William Shakespeare.

Chapter 5

SHAKESPEARE had settled down with a single acting company, and he stayed with them for the rest of his career; but he had not settled down as a writer. He went on experimenting with increasing vigor, trying first one kind of play and then another, and the plays he gave his fortunate company at the rate of two a year had no pattern and no neatness. They began to cover larger and larger areas of human experience, until in the end Shakespeare had brought the whole world into existence on the London stage.

One of the earliest plays that Shakespeare wrote for his new company was *King John*. History plays were extremely popular and the acting companies produced a great many of them, with sceptres and crowns as part of their standard stage equipment. The kings were usually as wooden as their sceptres, and King John is no exception. But Shakespeare's tremendous knowledge of people was beginning to show even as early as this. There is Arthur, with his touching small-boy courage; there is his sharp-tongued mother Constance; and above all, there is the delightful Faulconbridge, who moves through the pageantry and speech-making with a cheerful, impudent realism.

> 'Zounds! I was never so bethumped with words
> Since I first called my brother's father dad.

An Introduction to Shakespeare

King John is an historical pageant, with no central point of interest, but *Richard III* is a melodrama with a towering villain. Audience after audience must have leaned forward, tense with excitement, waiting for the "foul bunch-backed toad" to be finally destroyed, and Richard Burbage played the brilliant, evil, unhappy hunchback with what was apparently startling force. It was, moreover, a play that lent itself to effective staging, especially in the scene where "the lights burn blue" and the ghosts of the murdered dead rise from the ground to file past King Richard's tent.

To a London audience of Shakespeare's day the play would be a part of their living past, for Richard's successor was their own Queen's grandfather. Shakespeare himself was a householder in the parish where Richard had lodged when he came to London, and the past seemed as real and near to him as it did to his audience. In fact, Shakespeare made his own view of history so vivid and convincing that the average person takes his impression of the kings of England from him rather than from sober historians.

For his next history play Shakespeare went back to an earlier king of the same name. *Richard II* also centers around a single figure, but this time the king does not dominate the action. He is not a man of action at all. He is one of those people who constantly dramatize themselves and see themselves moving through life as tragic heroes. They cannot achieve anything, because they are too fascinated by their own reaction to events to pay much attention to the events themselves. When Richard's officers bring him news of a revolt, the average king would have buckled on his sword; Richard launches into a delicate, brilliant, self-pitying account of the hollowness of royal majesty:

An Introduction to Shakespeare

For God's sake, let us sit upon the ground
And tell sad stories of the death of kings . . .

Richard almost enjoyed his own deposition, since he was able to put such pathos into the situation. He was authentically a martyr, but he could not help taking an aesthetic interest in his martyrdom.

When *Richard II* was put into print the deposition scene had to be omitted, because Queen Elizabeth did not wish her subjects to read anything that described a monarch losing his crown. But otherwise there was no need to censor any of Shakespeare's plays, for he always wrote as a loyal subject and a good Englishman. It is in *Richard II*, in fact, that England is given its most beautiful tribute.

> This royal throne of kings, this sceptered isle,
> This earth of majesty, this seat of Mars,
> This other Eden, demi-paradise . . .
> This happy breed of men, this little world,
> This precious stone set in the silver sea . . .
> This blessed plot, this earth, this realm, this England . . .
> This land of such dear souls, this dear, dear land . . .

Shakespeare loved England, and this is one of the reasons why England has always so deeply loved Shakespeare.

In the last act of *Richard II* the new king, Henry IV, is shown worrying about his son, for young Prince Hal has been spending his time in taverns with "loose companions." The next play in the series, *Henry IV*, starts with the same situation. Then, in scene two, the leader of the "loose companions" comes onstage, and one of the world's greatest comic creations leaps into full life and into immortality.

An Introduction to Shakespeare

Sir John Falstaff is one of the most outrageous individuals who ever set an audience laughing as soon as they looked at him. Old, fat and permanently bankrupt, he sails through the play with a cheerful lack of morals that brings him into constant and violent conflict with the law. It is the law that is wrong in Falstaff's opinion. He is above the law. And the average London audience, hemmed in by a succession of rules and regulations every day of their lives, rocked with helpless mirth while Falstaff made his enthusiastic progress over the corpses of dignity, respectability and virtuous living.

Falstaff was a captain in the army, but he was also a complete realist. His idea was to let everyone else get killed, if they must, but he saw no reason to involve himself in anything so unpleasant. Most Elizabethans, on the stage at least, rushed into battle with swords waving and banners flying, to prove their honor against the foe or die in the attempt. Falstaff, on the other hand, approached the day of battle with frank misgivings: "I would it were bedtime, Hal, and all well." Falstaff told lies of such intricacy and towering magnificence that anyone might be awed into preferring them to the simple truth, and yet he could be honest enough when he wanted to be. In fact, he is one of the most honest men who ever waddled into immortality, and even the people who disapprove of him cannot help loving the old sinner.

Shakespeare had an extraordinary capacity for presenting people as they were, without commenting on them or taking sides, and he could put into the same play two men as unlike as Falstaff and Hotspur. While Falstaff is the complete realist about war, Hotspur is the complete romantic, and a whole generation of impressionable Elizabethan apprentices went around quoting his speech on honor:

44

An Introduction to Shakespeare

By heaven, methinks it were an easy leap
To pluck bright honor from the pale-faced moon . . .

Even Prince Hal, who tried to take a reasonable position some-where in the middle, could not help feeling that Hotspur overdid his enthusiasm—"he that kills me some six or seven dozen of Scots at a breakfast, washes his hands, and says to his wife, 'Fie upon this quiet life! I want work.'" Yet Hotspur is a charming human being, with his excitability and his warmth and his delightful gift of teasing, and Shakespeare understood him just as well as he understood Falstaff. The two men could never have understood each other, but there was room for them both in the wide universe of Shakespeare's mind.

Shakespeare developed as a playwright with tremendous speed. Once he knew what he wanted to say he found out very quickly how to say it, and only a few years separate the stiff, careful pageantry of *King John* from the vigor and hu-manity of *Henry IV*. What was true of his history plays was equally true of his comedies, in which he moved with the same giant strides towards reality.

The first of these comedies was probably *The Taming of the Shrew*, which, like *King John*, was an adaptation of an older play. Shakespeare took what was originally a tidy little farce and transformed it into a vigorous and colorful one. But it remains a rather heartless play, and although Katharina and Petruchio are entertaining they are not particularly real people. After that, Shakespeare wrote no more farces. A farce depends on situation rather than characterization and gives very little room for the development of real human beings.

Shakespeare used another old plot in his comedy of *The Two Gentlemen of Verona*, or rather, he used an accumulation of plot situations. These situations had been used for decades in the Italian drama, and English audiences were familiar with them in both books and plays. There were the stock devices of the girl dressed as a boy, the noble band of outlaws, the sheltering forest, the helpful friar, the ladder of cords, the exile from Court, the girl talking over her lover with her maid, and the girl dressed as a page who pleads her lover's suit with her rival. Shakespeare never tried to be particularly original in his plots and he lavishly used all these old devices in the same play, but he brought a kind of gaiety to the worn-out situations that went a long way towards bringing them back to life.

A love comedy of this type depends on a special convention that everyone recognized in Shakespeare's day. It was the convention that set so many young Elizabethans to writing sonnets, brooding over flowers, or changing their hose three times a day in the hope of pleasing their beloveds. The emotion was not new then, any more than it is now, but in Shakespeare's day all young men in love were supposed to behave in exactly the same fashion. The paintings of the period are full of lovesick young gentlemen, leaning against trees with their hands on their silken hearts or posed in noble desolation with the fires of love raging behind them; and most of the poetry of the day, lovely as it is, is one long wail against the hardness of some lady's heart.

Shakespeare's two gentlemen of Verona are conventionally lovesick young Elizabethans, and if the play were no more profound than its heroes it would be only a piece of fashionable thistledown. But the women in the play are more interesting. Silvia is a delightful girl—honorable, cheerful and intelligent—and she sets the note for the heroines in Shakespeare's later comedies. They have more sense than the heroes, and they are much better company.

The play has its song, since a comedy without music would have been unthinkable.

> Who is Silvia? what is she?
> That all our swains commend her?

It also has its clowns, since the audience expected them and Shakespeare never disappointed his audience. Shakespeare's clowns are usually one of two kinds, the wise clown who is generally a court jester and a sophisticate, and the rustic clown, who means well but is not very bright. Having included everything else in *The Two Gentlemen of Verona*, Shakespeare also included both kinds of clowns. Speed, with his sharp tongue and his gift of words, is the first dim showing-forth of the line that develops into Feste and Lear's tragic fool, while Launce, with his solemn and useless efforts to be intelligent, is the forerunner of Dogberry and the wonderful Bottom.

In another of his comedies, *The Merchant of Venice*, Shakespeare uses many of the Italian plot devices over again: the lovesick young man, the comic servant, the exchange of rings, the girl dressed as a boy, and the heroine discussing her lover's qualifications with her maid. In the case of any other writer but Shakespeare this might have resulted in a tired copy of his previous comedy, but in Shakespeare's case it flowered into something altogether original and brilliant. *The Merchant of Venice* is one of the most popular plays he ever wrote, and generations of theatregoers have fallen in love with Portia. She is one of the most charming women who ever walked out of a dramatist's script and into reality—a great lady with a strong sense of fun, a profound sense of honor, and the wonderful gift of not taking herself too seriously.

The other important character in the play is Shylock, the Jew of Venice, and here again, as in the case of the lovesick young men, the point of view of the period must be remembered. In Shakespeare's day it was considered quite legitimate to kill a man if you did not like his religion. The Protestants killed the Catholics and the Catholics killed the Protestants, and the fact that they both called themselves Christians made no difference to them.

The only time the Protestants and Catholics of the period were united was when they turned on the only other religion that also worshipped one God. This was the religion of the Jews, and all the Christians of Shakespeare's day persecuted the Jews. On the Continent they were forced to wear special clothes and live in special quarters of town, and they were exiled from England altogether. Tales circulated in England that the Jews were poisoners and killed children, and when Christopher Marlowe wrote *The Jew of Malta* he showed the leading character embarking on a career of wholesale slaughter which was accepted by the audience as entirely natural.

Shakespeare, like Marlowe, had been brought up to believe a legend about the Jews, but there was something in Shakespeare that made it impossible for him to believe the ancient and evil lie. Shylock was a human being to Shakespeare, and he could not make his mind follow a pre-arranged pattern when he thought about human beings. "I am a Jew. Hath not a Jew eyes? hath not a Jew hands, organs, dimensions, senses, affections, passions? fed with the same food, hurt with the same weapons, subject to the same diseases, healed by the same means, warmed and cooled by the same winter and summer as a Christian is? If you prick us, do we not bleed? if you tickle us, do we not laugh? if you poison us, do we not die? and if you wrong us, shall we not revenge?" Portia's speech on justice is a beautiful thing and worthy to be admired, but Shylock's speech on justice is a more remarkable achievement. For once an Elizabethan was able to break through the shackles of his religious education, and the lines are a triumph not only for Shakespeare but for the fundamental spirit of human brotherhood.

One of the most interesting things about *The Merchant of Venice* is Shakespeare's use of poetry as a tool for his stage-craft. The last scene is supposed to take place by moonlight, and yet Shakespeare's company had to play this scene on an open stage around four o'clock in the afternoon. The only way that Shakespeare could persuade his audience to come to moonlit Belmont was through his use of words:

> How sweet the moonlight sleeps upon this bank!
> Here will we sit and let the sounds of music
> Creep in our ears; soft stillness and the night
> Become the touches of sweet harmony.
> Sit, Jessica; look, how the floor of heaven
> Is thick inlaid with patines of bright gold . . .

The willing audience listened, and entered a moonlit park, for there is nothing the imagination cannot do if a great poet knows how to arouse it.

Another comedy, *A Midsummer Night's Dream*, is all moonlight, with a touch of moonshine. It is the most enchanting fairy tale ever written and yet it reflects with cheerful fidelity the villagers and cowslips and hedgehogs of the ordinary English countryside. It is like looking at the world upside down in a sheet of water. All the familiar things are there but, like Bottom, they are translated.

No one but Shakespeare would have set someone like Bottom in fairyland. For Bottom was a weaver and of a practical nature, and in any other hands but Shakespeare's he would have trampled on the delicate fabric of the play. But Bottom, helpfully instructing a fairy how to attack a "red-hipped humble-bee on the top of a thistle" and the exact way to carry home the honey-bag, shows a bland dignity that is quite undisturbed by the fact he happens at the moment to be ornamented with an ass's head and a wreath of musk-roses.

A Midsummer Night's Dream reaches its climax in the play that is acted before Duke Theseus, with Bottom heading the cast. All England was in the grip of these well-intentioned local amateur theatricals, which seemed even funnier then than they do now; for the old plays that were still being acted had a stiff elegance and an impassioned melancholy that made them a little ridiculous even when they were properly presented. A play like *Appius and Virginia* was advertised as a "tragical comedy" and its long lines wailed like a defective bagpipe.

O man, O mould, O muck, O clay! O hell, O hellish hound.
O false Judge Appius, rabbling wretch, is this thy treason found?

It needed only the most delicate touch to push this sort of thing into the realm of outright comedy, and Shakespeare supplied it in the "very tragical mirth" of Bottom's conscientious production of Pyramus and Thisbe. The gallant little troupe in their solemn performance before Duke Theseus present the funniest tragedy that ever brought tears of helpless mirth to the eyes of the audience.

An Introduction to Shakespeare

Shakespeare had used the device before in *Love's Labour's Lost*, where a group of amateurs inch their way through a show, pausing at times to argue with their noble listeners; but what had been merely charmingly effective in the earlier play becomes a comic masterpiece in the *Dream*. Yet, however Shakespeare may smile at Bottom and his earnest fellow actors, the great actor-dramatist did not really feel superior to them. "The best in this kind are but shadows, and the worst are no worse, if imagination amend them." It is part of Shakespeare's great strength as a writer that he never felt superior to anyone, and he kept a gentle courtesy in his point of view even towards fools.

This same gentleness on Shakespeare's part shows in his attitude towards the earlier writers from whom he took the plots of some of his plays. He could pick up a rather foolish play or poem, read it with great care, ignore its foolishness for the little of value there might be in it, and then transform it into a masterpiece.

For instance, at about this time Shakespeare read a popular poem by Arthur Brooke on the tragedy of two young lovers named Romeus and Juliet. Brooke was retelling an old Italian story, and he used an extraordinary style that compares quite favorably with Bottom's. This, according to Brooke, is Juliet's behavior in the potion scene:

Her dainty tender parts gan shiver all for dread,
Her golden hairs did stand upright upon her chillish head . . .

Shakespeare took Brooke's stuffed characters and transformed them into real people, he took the pretentious verse and transmuted it into golden poetry, and he made *Romeo and Juliet* into one of the most loved plays ever written. Brooke's tragedy was meaningless because there was no special reason why it should have happened, but Shakespeare made it into a tragedy of haste. He emphasizes the sense of hurry by making Juliet younger than she was in the original version and condensing the action into less than a week. Even the weather is hot, and an atmosphere of quick-flowering beauty and early death is the background that is created for the story of the immortal and tragic lovers.

A lesser writer than Shakespeare might have tried to keep the play to a single note of lyric love. But Shakespeare, who had thrust a weaver into fairyland, had no hesitation about putting a couple of cheerful realists into *Romeo and Juliet*. Mercutio and Juliet's nurse do not weaken the tragedy; they enrich it, in the usual astonishing fashion of Shakespeare's comedians. Mercutio is a humorist by intention; he is a subtle and intelligent young man who knows exactly how entertaining he is, and the fact that he "loves to hear himself talk" is only proof of his good judgment. The Nurse, on the other hand, does not mean to be funny. She feels she is a very sober, sensible, practical woman and she has no idea what actually happens every time she opens her mouth. Shakespeare had no objection to laughter in his tragedies. The two elements combine in real life and they were free to combine in his plays also.

None of these plays that Shakespeare wrote in the early years of the Chamberlain's company was mentioned by the critics who had lavished such praise on *Venus and Adonis* and *Lucrece*. But in the fourth year of the company's existence a London writer undertook a survey of the current literary scene and for the first time Shakespeare was singled out as a major playwright.

An Introduction to Shakespeare

The name of this London writer was Francis Meres, and he had been commissioned by a local publisher to write the book for an educational series. Many people felt that literature was something that had been produced only by the Greeks and Romans, but Meres knew that literature was a living thing and could happen anywhere. He was convinced that many modern Englishmen wrote "gorgeous and delectable" verse, and one of the best of these, in his opinion, was William Shakespeare.

Meres mentions Shakespeare under five different headings in his little book. He lists him among the lyric poets, the tragic dramatists, the comic dramatists and the love poets and then devotes a long section to discussing his work as a whole. "The sweet witty soul of Ovid lies in mellifluous and honey-tongued Shakespeare, witness his *Venus and Adonis*, his *Lucrece*, his sugared sonnets among his private friends. As Plautus and Seneca are accounted the best for comedy and tragedy among the Latins, so Shakespeare among the English is the most excellent in both kinds for the stage." Meres then continues with a list of the plays Shakespeare had written and ends with the statement that if the Muses spoke English they would use language like his.

Meres did not hold a very distinguished position in literary circles, and his praise of Shakespeare's plays would not have carried any weight at the universities. He wrote his little book for the guidance of middle-class readers in London, and they already knew Shakespeare and loved him. Still, they must have been pleased to have Francis Meres confirm their own judgment and to know the next time they laughed with Falstaff or wept with Juliet that they were not only enjoying themselves but encouraging a major English playwright.

Chapter 6

ALL THESE plays of Shakespeare's were presented by the same group of actors—Burbage, Shakespeare, Heminges, Kempe and the rest—working together with increasing skill and experience, and it is possible to trace, in a general way, how each play was produced.

An acting company usually chose a play by having it read to them in an alehouse by the author. The actors paid for the drinks and bought the play if they liked it, and the author usually had nothing more to do with it. But Shakespeare was an actor as well as an author and he was involved with all the production details that followed.

The first problem in producing a play was to get the script approved by the government. Queen Elizabeth did not want any unpatriotic material to creep into the plays, and a special censor read every play in London before it could be presented on the stage. Sometimes so many lines had to be omitted that the play could not be produced at all, but in the case of a script by Shakespeare there were probably only a few minor alterations.

When the script came back to the theatre with the censor's initials on the last page, it was stitched together and bound in heavier paper so that it would not wear out. This was the official copy and the joint, permanent copy of the actors. It was then given to the copyist who wrote out each character's part on a separate roll, indicating the cue by giving the end of the preceding speech and showing the action in the lefthand margin. Until the part was memorized the actor kept the roll in his hand as he worked, and in the case of a long part like Falstaff's the roll would be his close companion for some time.

The next problem was casting, but this was not a difficult one for a brilliant, versatile, highly trained group of men who were also close friends, especially since the play had been written by one of their own number. There was no star system and each actor took the part that would be best for the play as a whole. Will Kempe, for instance, was the most famous comedian in England, but in *Romeo and Juliet* he took the comparatively small part of Peter. The chief comedy part in the play is of course the Nurse, and that was possibly played by Thomas Pope, who was a very famous comedian in his own day. But whether Pope or another, it would be whatever actor had been decided upon by the company as a whole, and the same thing would apply to Shakespeare's roles also. He was not an "immortal bard" in those days. He was a working actor, cooperating with other actors, and if he had not wanted it to be that way he would never have joined the Chamberlain's company.

The heroine of the play—Juliet, Portia, Silvia or whoever she might be—was played by a boy whose voice had not yet changed. These boys came into the company young, chosen for their good looks, their intelligence and their grace, and each one had been taken into the home of one of the leading actors as an apprentice. John Heminges, for instance, taught the difficult art of stagecraft to boys like Alexander Cooke and John Rice while Rebecca Heminges kept them well fed and happy and brought them up with her own fourteen children. The boys worked hard in the theatre, since they were constantly under the supervision of a group of experienced adults, and their acting was so brilliant that Shakespeare could create any kind of a heroine and know that the part would be well played.

The average Elizabethan boy, in the theatre or out of it, was not like the average boy of today. He had been taught to handle his body gracefully, to dance and write poetry and sing, and the men of the period wore silks and velvets and perfumes as much as the women did. Even their clothes were rather like the women's, rigid and jeweled and ornamental with heavy ruffs and stiffened doublets, except that the men wore trunk hose and the women wore farthingales. An Elizabethan boy in a wig and a farthingale could, as Shakespeare said,

> well usurp the grace,
> Voice, gait and action of a gentlewoman.

In fact, when an English traveller of the period returned from Italy, he reported with some astonishment that the Italian actresses were nearly as effective on the stage as the London boys.

Most of the minor speaking parts could be handled by doubling, and extra actors at a shilling a day were hired to be the Venetian magnificoes in *The Merchant of Venice*, the soldiers in *Richard II* or the guests at the ball in *Romeo and Juliet*. These actors, like the boy apprentices, had nothing to do but to learn their parts and work hard at rehearsals, but the company sharers like Burbage and Shakespeare and Heminges were responsible for all the other production details that had to be attended to before the play could open.

The most expensive single item was the costuming, and an acting company had to be both alert and experienced to keep down costs in this department. There was no special effort at realism, and both King John and Duke Theseus probably walked the stage in Elizabethan doublets. On the other hand, the actors could hardly be expected to appear in ordinary street clothes and give an illusion of far-off times and distant places, and the problem was solved by the use of extremely beautiful and expensive fabrics. An actors' inventory of the period is a riot of color: a scarlet cloak with gold laces and buttons, a crimson velvet jerkin with blue satin sleeves, purple hose embroidered with silver. Every company had piles of old costumes stored away to be remodeled for the minor parts and for group scenes, but the actors who took the main roles evidently had their costumes designed for them at considerable expense. Gold lace was lavishly applied to their costumes, with copper lace for the lesser actors, and one London company ran up enormous bills with "the copper lace man."

In general, Shakespeare's comedies would not have been expensive to costume but his history plays were a different matter. History plays were always expensive to produce, with their large casts and elaborate costumes, especially since some armor had to be rented also. An especially costly scene would have been the deposition scene in *Richard II*, with actors dressed as bishops and lords and abbots crowding the stage.

The stage sets were less complicated than the costumes, since so much was left to the imagination. In Shakespeare's boyhood the actors apparently used to indicate a change of scene with a printed placard: "This is a street," "This is Persia," and so on. But they soon found they could trust the intelligence of the audience if the dialogue was well written. Shakespeare's words could create the Capulet orchard much more effectively than a painter could put fruit trees on a canvas, and in any case the large painted back-drops that were so popular in the Italian theatre would not have been practical on the open-air Elizabethan stage.

Stage properties were another matter, since they were expected to be as realistic as paint and ingenuity could make them. Here again, however, a great deal of money could be saved by using old properties over again. The storage rooms of Shakespeare's company housed a magnificent clutter of objects which could be searched through for each new play. Juliet's bed, for instance, would have been an easy enough matter; the company probably had several beds, any one of which could be repainted and given a new coverlet. And, if they wished to be specially economical, they could even give Juliet the tomb that they had used for *Titus Andronicus.*

A special order would have to be sent to the property man for the ass's head that Bottom wears in *A Midsummer Night's Dream;* and the severed head in *King John* would have to be realistically carved and colored to resemble the actor who played the unlucky Duke of Austria. But, in general, Shakespeare's plays did not put much of a burden on the properties department. *The Two Gentlemen of Verona*, for instance, calls for very little beyond a letter and a glove. Many of the plays of the period call for complicated and expensive properties like dragons and steeples and rainbows, and one company even owned a large and realistic cloud that was backed by a board and pulled around on wires. Shakespeare did not use much of this sort of thing in his plays, partly because he did

An Introduction to Shakespeare

not use the mythological backgrounds that were so beloved in his period. A rival company had to invest in expensive items like Cerberus' head and Phaeton's chariot, Mercury's wings and Iris' rainbow, but Shakespeare kept to earth in his plays and probably saved his company a good deal of money in the process.

In the meantime rehearsals had been progressing steadily and the play was taking shape in the actors' minds. The men who took the parts of Falstaff and Richard and Mercutio were the best in the business, with voices trained as accurately as singers to handle the loveliness of the verse. And if there was anything they did not understand about the characterization they had one advantage that no actor has ever had since: they could ask Shakespeare himself for advice and help on the subject.

Rehearsals were conducted in a businesslike manner, with an actor fined if he were late or absent, and an action sheet was worked out and hung on a peg near the stage so that each man would know the exact time of his entrances and exits. There had to be special dance rehearsals for the actors who appeared at the ball in *Romeo and Juliet* or for the children who played the fairies in *A Midsummer Night's Dream*. The boy who acted Arthur in *King John* would need special training for the long jump he had to take from the balcony to the stage, and the actors who played the ghosts in *Richard III* had to work out a careful system of timing for their entrance through the trapdoor. Someone even had to be responsible for the trained dog in *The Two Gentlemen of Verona* and for making sure that Romeo's page did not get onstage without his wrenching iron; and, however carefully the work might be divided up, it would be the business of the actor-managers to see that all the small details were attended to. Shakespeare and Burbage and Kempe and Heminges were directly responsible for the production as a whole, and they had to watch the multitude of minor details that in time would flow together into a smooth and successful performance.

An advertisement for the play was written out and sent to a printer named James Roberts who made up a sheaf of playbills that could be fastened up on posts around town. The man who sold the fruit and nuts laid in a new stock, since the opening of a new play usually brought an extra crowd of customers, and the company ran up their silk playing flag on the top turret. The first comers got the best seats, and the theatre began filling as much as two hours before the play would begin. The audience was a splendidly mixed crowd of people —workmen, housewives, children, young men from the law schools, lords, courting couples, apprentices, businessmen and anyone else who had an extra penny or two and could get away from work.

It was a large, restless, excitable, opinionated audience, and if it disapproved of a play it did not hesitate to let the actors know. In that case all the hard work that had gone into the show was a complete loss and it was never presented again. Sometimes the audience liked a play fairly well and it would be given two or three more times that season. And sometimes the audience greeted it with complete enthusiasm and the play went into the permanent repertoire of the company, to be played over and over again in London and to be taken into the country each summer when the company toured. It was the custom to end each play with a leading actor coming forward in costume and requesting applause—Puck performs this service, for instance, in *A Midsummer Night's Dream*—and it must have been a wonderful moment for the actors when a roar of answering applause came from all sides of the theatre.

Echoes of this applause have still come down to us after more than three hundred years. There was such excitement over the scene in *Richard III* in which Burbage shouted, "A horse! a horse! my kingdom for a horse!" that the line became a slang phrase and was freely parodied by other playwrights. Falstaff's views on honor were quoted in a theatregoer's private correspondence, and *Romeo and Juliet* was so popular with young people that a writer of the period maintained that one young man's conversation was "naught but pure Juliet and Romeo." It was plays like these that paid the bills sent in by the costumers and painters and made up for the company's occasional failures.

It was also plays like these that were chosen for the annual theatre season at Court before Queen Elizabeth. The Queen did not go to the public theatres but she was nevertheless an ardent playgoer, and once a year the London actors went through the long, strenuous process of getting ready a series of plays for the Christmas season at Court.

The process started in the autumn, when the various acting companies of London loaded their wagons with costumes and properties, collected their musicians and travelled out to the western suburb of Clerkenwell to give a series of full-dress performances before Edmund Tilney, the Master of the Revels. Tilney and his assistants chose the plays which they felt the Queen would like best and then had them "corrected and amended" so that nothing unsuitable would be spoken before the royal majesty of England. The plays had already been rehearsed for regular London production, but as soon as the scripts had been approved they were rehearsed all over again.

An Introduction to Shakespeare

These Court rehearsals were conducted at Clerkenwell at night, after the regular working day of the London actors was over, and the Office of the Revels ran up a heavy bill for candles and torches to light the hall and for firewood and coal to keep the actors warm. The performances before the Queen were presented in a lighted hall at night instead of on an outdoor stage in the afternoon, and everything was on a more formal and elaborate scale. Painted sets were used, for instance, and the designers were expected not only to be well informed on the laws of perspective but also to have "some smack of geometry," since they had to create an illusion of streets and houses with nothing but painted canvas from the linen-draper's.

The costumes were even more splendid than those in the public theatres, and piles of velvet and damask and cloth of gold, silk fringes and silver laces, were delivered to the Office of the Revels. The Office bought buttons by the gross and had standing orders with embroiderers and tailors to do the work in their own homes if there was too much to be handled out at Clerkenwell. There were experts to curl the silk wigs and to make beards, white, black and auburn, at about a shilling apiece. Even gloves were bought by the dozen, for an actor could not appear ungloved before the Queen. The property-makers collected piles of brown paper and plaster-of-paris to be transformed into a dazzling array of fruits and flowers and mountains and whatever else the plays required, and even the wool that was used for stuffing the fishes cost twelvepence. Moreover the Revels Office, like every other theatrical venture, was never ready quite on time, so that a special bonus had to be given if the workers went without their dinner or were kept up all night.

An Introduction to Shakespeare

The climax of all this activity came on the evening of the 26th of December, when the theatre season opened at Court. The honor of appearing on the opening date usually went to Shakespeare's company, not only because they had some of the best actors and the best plays in London but also because the patron of the company was the Queen's cousin and, as Lord Chamberlain, had the Office of the Revels under his direct control.

It must have been a rather frightening experience for an actor to appear for the first time before Queen Elizabeth. She was one of the greatest monarchs in the world, and she moved in a glitter of gold and jewels among the bowed figures of her courtiers. She sat like an aging hawk, with her long nose and brilliant eyes, waiting for the Chamberlain's men to entertain her, and the actor who came onstage to recite the Prologue might have been forgiven if his legs shook a little under his robe.

Yet, under her formidable exterior Queen Elizabeth was the ideal playgoer. In spite of over sixty years of a tense and exhausting life she had kept her lively capacity for enjoyment, and she shared with the Londoners a wholehearted enthusiasm for a good play. She had endured a great many amateur stage productions as she went around England on her progresses and had listened patiently to local schoolmasters who forgot their carefully rehearsed speeches and university lecturers who remembered them all too well. But she still remained ready to enjoy herself and to applaud a good show whenever it came her way.

All the London acting companies owed a great debt to Queen Elizabeth. Time and again the mayor of London tried to close the theatres and in each case he was stopped by the

Queen, who said that the London theatres had to remain open or the actors would get no training for their annual Christmas season at Court. Shakespeare's company could not have stayed in existence if it had not been for the sheltering hand of the Queen, and none of Shakespeare's plays would ever have been produced if Elizabeth had disliked the theatre.

Chapter 7

THE FIRST four years of Shakespeare's company were not easy ones. England was in the midst of a business depression which had been complicated by several seasons of heavy rains and bad harvests. In *A Midsummer Night's Dream*, Shakespeare blames the bad weather on a war between the fairy king and queen but he gives a realistic enough description of its results.

> ... the green corn
> Hath rotted ere his youth attained a beard;
> The fold stands empty in the drowned field,
> And crows are fatted with the murrion flock ...

A luxury trade like the theatre was among the first to feel the effects of the depression, and the atmosphere was very unlike the free-spending days in which James Burbage had built his Theatre.

Nevertheless, the Chamberlain's company made money, even in those difficult times, and the actors in it prospered. They used their extra income in various ways, and Shakespeare used his to enhance the family position in Stratford. Two years after he joined the company he bought his father a coat-of-arms, and the following spring he bought the second largest house in Stratford for his family.

An Introduction to Shakespeare

When William Shakespeare was twelve years old his father had applied for a coat-of-arms and for some reason had not been granted it. During the following years John Shakespeare had to watch the sons of his friends achieve high positions in Stratford while his own eldest son worked as a common actor on the London stage. It must have been a source of great satisfaction to both men when William Shakespeare obtained a coat-of-arms for his father and John Shakespeare was able to walk the streets of Stratford as an Elizabethan gentleman with a silver falcon for his crest.

The purchase of a house also added a great deal to the prestige of the Shakespeare family in Stratford. The building was called New Place, and Shakespeare got it cheap because it was not in good repair. But it was a beautiful residence, built by a one-time mayor of London, and its owner was even entitled to a special pew in the Stratford church.

A year later Shakespeare made an even more important investment, but this time it was not in Stratford but in London. Many actors bought coats-of-arms, and many bought houses, but Shakespeare was one of the first to help buy a theatre.

What had happened was that Shakespeare's fellow actor, Richard Burbage, was in serious difficulties. Richard and his brother Cuthbert had inherited the Theatre when their father died, and with it the complicated legal burdens that James Burbage had accumulated in the course of his stormy career. The lease had expired on the land on which the Theatre was built and the landlord suddenly decided he would tear the building down. Richard and Cuthbert Burbage had inherited their father's temperament and were not easily defeated; they decided they would dismantle the Theatre and rebuild it somewhere else.

An Introduction to Shakespeare

A plan of this kind required money, and Cuthbert and Richard did not have enough. Their father, two years earlier, had spent a great deal of money on a theatre called the Black-friars on the west side of town, which he had never been able to open, and the family was at the moment very short of cash. So Richard turned to his fellow actors of the Chamberlain's company and made an arrangement with them that was alto-gether new in the history of the English theatre. Shakespeare, Heminges, Kempe, Phillips and Pope each agreed to put up an equal sum of money to finance the rebuilding of the theatre and in turn they each owned one-tenth of it. The Burbage brothers owned the remaining half, having raised the money for the other five shares by borrowing from a friend. Actors had frequently been sharers in a company, with joint owner-ship of scripts and costumes and properties, but this was the first time they had become sharers in a theatre. The plan might not have worked with ordinary men, but the men of this group were all close friends and could trust each other. Cuthbert Burbage put it this way: "To ourselves we joined those deserving men, Shakespeare, Heminges . . . and others, partners in the profits." They were also partners in the risk, and in the winter of 1598 the risk must often have looked larger than any possible profits.

The first problem facing the new syndicate was to lease a plot of ground on which to locate the theatre. Because of the opposition of the mayor they could not build anywhere in London but they finally found a piece of land across the river in Southwark, not very far from the Rose theatre, and took it on a thirty-one-year lease.

The next problem was to dismantle the Theatre. The land-lord wanted to keep the valuable lumber for his own use and had posted agents to guard it, but three days after Christmas the Burbage brothers arrived on the grounds accompanied by their remarkable mother and a London carpenter named Peter Street. Street brought with him a crew of workmen armed with wrecking tools, and the landlord later claimed they also brought along swords and daggers. He even tried to sue them for trampling on the grass, but the Burbages emerged in triumph with the lumber and they later won the suit also. The theatre was theirs, although the land was not, and Peter Street carried it down in sections to his wharf on the Thames and ferried it over to Southwark.

Since the theatre was going to a new location, the syndicate decided to give it a new name. They named it the Globe and were determined to make it the finest theatre building in London.

The valuable timber of the Theatre had been taken down carefully and could be fitted back into place to form the framework of the Globe. About four hundred pounds had to be spent in new fittings and for the wages of carpenters, plasterers and painters, as well as for the heavy piles that had to be sunk to keep the theatre steady in the marshy soil of Southwark. This money was contributed equally by the various members of the syndicate, but Shakespeare seems to have been regarded as the leader. When a legal survey was made of the land on which the Globe stood it was described as being in the possession of "William Shakespeare and others."

The district in Southwark in which the Globe had been erected was near the river and was consequently called the Bankside. It was a colorful, lively part of town and had been a theatrical district since the days of the first of the bear gardens. A great many actors lived in the Bankside area, and

An Introduction to Shakespeare

Shakespeare himself was a resident taxpayer there at about the time the Globe opened. Most of the audience came from the London side of the river, and they were rowed over in cushioned boats at inexpensive rates by the watermen.

There was a great improvement in the income of the watermen when the splendid new theatre ran up its playing flag and opened for business. The Globe was called "the glory of the Bank" and it had a right to the name. Not only was it the handsomest theatre in town but all of Shakespeare's plays were produced in it from that time forward.

One of the first plays to be presented at the Globe was Shakespeare's new history play of *Henry V*. The play is an epic of local patriotism, full of flags and drums and trumpets, and again the line is clearly drawn between the gallant English and the feeble-minded French. The London audiences were currently in a state of martial excitement because the Earl of Essex had just set out with a glittering array to subdue the Irish, and since they did not know how badly Essex was going to fare in Ireland they were happily convinced that any sort of invasion was legitimate and that any Englishman was a match for ten foreigners.

Shakespeare was a poet and he gave this single-minded patriotism a kind of beauty of its own, rising to a climax in King Henry's speech at Agincourt. Most of his history plays contain battle orations, from Talbot's speech in *Henry VI* to Richmond's in *Richard III*, but they lack the authentic passion of Henry's speech to his soldiers:

> We few, we happy few, we band of brothers;
> For he today that sheds his blood with me
> Shall be my brother . . .

An Introduction to Shakespeare

Yet, as usual, Shakespeare was able to see the other side of the question. Falstaff, that great realist, was dead, and his prose epitaph is the most wonderful thing in the play. Yet there are other soldiers in *Henry V*, not knights like Sir John Falstaff but ordinary infantry. In particular there is Michael Williams, who is not sure that there is a real reason for invading France. "I am afeard there are few die well that die in a battle; for how can they charitably dispose of anything when blood is their argument? Now, if these men do not die well, it will be a black matter for the king that led them to it." Here is Shakespeare again, refusing to look at things with the eyes of his times and no more content to romanticize war than he was to villify the Jews. Shakespeare had encountered a great many old soldiers in London, since the city supplied a quarter of England's army, and he knew that war was not quite the glorious affair that the Elizabethans had been brought up to believe.

It was also in the early days of the Globe that Shakespeare wrote his three romantic comedies: *Twelfth Night, As You Like It* and *Much Ado About Nothing.* All three have easygoing titles (*Twelfth Night* is subtitled *What You Will*) and all three have highly improbable plots. As one of the characters admitted with engaging candor, "If this were played upon a stage now, I could condemn it as an improbable fiction."

Nothing is more remarkable in Shakespeare than his ability to take confused plots and outworn situations and make them over into something altogether new and enchanting. *Twelfth Night* makes use of all the devices that were ancient when he wrote *The Two Gentlemen of Verona:* the lovesick hero wilting over his unapproachable lady, the girl dressed as a man who pleads her lover's suit with her rival, and even the device of the twins who are mistaken for each other that he used in *The Comedy of Errors*. It is partly Shakespeare's poetry that exalts this flimsy material, and it is partly his wonderful gift for creating real people. Viola's notions of how to behave as a boy are entirely her own, and like most of Shakespeare's heroines she knows how to make fun of herself. This is an art that the girls in the comedies possess naturally, while the men in the comedies learn it late or not at all. The most dignified male in the cast of *Twelfth Night* is Malvolio, and he is the butt of the whole play. Dignity does not thrive in a Shakespearean comedy.

As You Like It has an even more improbable plot than *Twelfth Night*. Shakespeare took it from a romance called *Rosalynde* that young Tom Lodge had written on shipboard many years earlier and which belonged to an old-fashioned type of fiction even then. English readers had been brought up on the Robin Hood legends, and Shakespeare's outlaws who lived in a "golden world" in the forest seemed natural enough to them. They were not even surprised by a lion roaming about or by the introduction of a symbolical character like Hymen, the god of marriage. But Shakespeare could take this outworn clutter of devices and make it another of his lovely sunlit plays, with one of the most charming heroines he ever created in Rosalind. Like Viola, Rosalind can laugh at herself, but she is more intelligent than Viola and her laughter is worth more. She shares Mercutio's theory that there is something essentially comic about the act of falling in love; but while Mercutio was able to view the whole business with the amused detachment of an outsider, Rosalind was fathoms deep in love herself and deserves a special salute from anyone who loves gallantry and a good wit.

An Introduction to Shakespeare

The third play of the series, *Much Ado About Nothing*, is not so much a comedy as a melodrama with two comic sub-plots. As a melodrama it is not a great success, and Shakespeare's title indicates that he did not take it very seriously, but his comedy situations are another matter entirely. The first of these is a word-duel between two young people named Benedick and Beatrice, who have a brisk contempt for love and for each other and who finally fall in love to their mutual surprise if not that of the audience. In the hands of the average playwright Beatrice would have been a shrew, pretty as she was; in Shakespeare's hands she is a cheerful wit who is thoroughly bored by the average man and prefers to have a good time by herself. As one character in the play remarks, "She is never sad but when she sleeps; and not ever sad then, for I have heard my daughter say, she hath often dreamed of unhappiness and waked herself with laughing."

The other comic sub-plot in the play concerns the two constables, Dogberry and Verges, who track down the villain. They do it quite by accident, for they are no brighter than Bottom. They are both men of determined and idiotic dignity, and good comic actors can do wonders with the parts. The Chamberlain's company had excellent actors, since Will Kempe played Dogberry and another experienced actor, Richard Cowley, played Verges. This bit of information has come down to us because the play was printed from a stage copy and the proof-reader forgot to change all the names. From the same source we know that Jack Wilson was the musician who sang, "Sigh no more, ladies," in the second act. All three comedies of course have songs. "O mistress mine! where are you roaming?" and "The wind and the rain" come from *Twelfth Night*, and "Under the greenwood tree" and "It was a lover and his lass" from *As You Like It*.

An Introduction to Shakespeare

Shakespeare wrote one other light comedy at about this time, but a very different one. Its heroes and heroines are not lords and ladies but ordinary English citizens, and *The Merry Wives of Windsor* is the only middle-class comedy Shakespeare ever wrote.

The Merry Wives of Windsor brings back a whole crowd of names from *Henry IV*—Falstaff, Pistol, Nym, Bardolph and Shallow—but Shakespeare is not really interested in any of them, not even Falstaff. What interests him are the two wives of Windsor, Mrs. Ford and Mrs. Page, two lively, intelligent women who have a mild contempt for most men and a warm admiration for each other. It cannot be said that they make fools of the men in the cast since the men are mostly fools already, but they supply expert assistance to a rowdy plot that has this for its main idea. Shakespeare seems to have been extremely interested in this period in friendships between women; and the charming relationship between Celia and Rosalind in *As You Like It*, so accustomed to each other's minds that they can say anything without fear of being misunderstood, is echoed in the relationship between Mrs. Ford and Mrs. Page. As Ford himself remarked rather snappishly, "I think, if your husbands were dead, you two would marry."

All these comedies might be called women's plays, since the women control the plots and are by far the most interesting people in them. When Shakespeare wrote a political play, the men came back into control as they did in *Henry V*. But this time Shakespeare left English history, and *Julius Caesar* is a Roman tragedy.

London audiences knew a good deal about Caesar, since his murder had been a popular subject in amateur theatricals. Some members of the audience might also have read Plutarch's

An Introduction to Shakespeare

Lives, which had recently been translated by an Elizabethan soldier and which contained a brilliant study of Caesar's downfall. But even the best-informed members of the audience must have been startled by what Shakespeare was able to do with the old story.

Julius Caesar is a play about politics; and since politics are made by men, it is a study of why men do things. In this case, it is the problem of why a group of enlightened citizens decide to commit a murder—what drives them to it and what happens afterwards—and Shakespeare understood so well the complication of good intentions and political expediency that can lead to disaster that his play is just as applicable to the twentieth century as it was to the sixteenth.

The central figure in the play is not Caesar, but his friend Brutus who kills him. Brutus feels that the end justifies the means and that since Caesar is a dictator it is necessary to kill him. He clings to the fact that he is only doing evil so that good may come of it, and in the end he plunges the whole country into civil war.

As for Caesar, Shakespeare had never encountered a dictator and yet he knew the type well. He knew the self-hypnosis that drove him to think he was above ordinary human weaknesses, and the rage his friends felt when they saw him behave like a god, when they knew all about his deaf ear and his love of flattery and the other things that made him an ordinary man. Caesar, as long as he is alive, is an ordinary man, with more conceit than most. Caesar murdered is a legend, and Brutus and his friends cannot kill it.

> O Julius Caesar! thou art mighty yet!
> Thy spirit walks abroad and turns our swords . . .

An Introduction to Shakespeare

The conspirators have no unifying idea to hold them together once they have killed Caesar, and the quarrel between Brutus and his best friend is a marvellous study of two well-intentioned men who are getting increasingly on each other's nerves. The only man who knows exactly what he wants to do is Antony, and his speech to the Romans over Caesar's dead body is a kind of handbook for all skillful political propagandists.

Julius Caesar was one of the first of Shakespeare's plays to be produced at the Globe. In the autumn of the year the theatre was built, a German tourist named Thomas Platter crossed the Thames with his friends after lunch "and there in the house with the thatched roof witnessed an excellent performance of the tragedy of the first emperor Julius Caesar." The only difficulty was that Platter did not understand any English, so that Shakespeare's subtle characterization and brilliant dialogue passed completely over his head.

Still, Platter had a very good time. He warmly approved of the system of charging a penny at the door for general admission, with an additional charge upstairs for "the most comfortable seats, which are cushioned." He liked the raised stage which could be seen from any part of the house. He liked the custom of selling food and drink to the audience during the performance, and he was deeply impressed by the magnificent costumes. The cast of fifteen gave what Platter called an "excellent" performance, and "when the play was over, they danced very marvellously and gracefully together." The Globe unquestionably gave its customers their full money's worth, and the seven men who owned the theatre fully deserved the success that had come to them.

Chapter 8

HEN Shakespeare stopped publishing poetry and joined the Chamberlain's company instead, it must have seemed for a time that he had cut himself off from his reading public. His plays belonged to his company, not to himself, and most acting companies did not like plays to be published in book form.

Nevertheless, a successful play usually found its way into print, and both *Titus Andronicus* and the second part of *Henry VI* were published the same year the company was formed. They were not issued in the handsome format of Shakespeare's poems but in cheap pamphlets, and since it was not the custom to mention the playwright's name they were issued anonymously.

Three years later *Richard II, Richard III* and *Romeo and Juliet* were also published without the author's name, although the publisher of *Romeo and Juliet* made special mention of the "great applause" the play had been getting.

The publisher of *Richard II* and *Richard III* was a man named Andrew Wise, and he matched his name. Both plays went into second editions almost at once and it occurred to Wise that a playwright's name evidently had some value in selling a book. Therefore in the second edition of both plays he added a new line to the title-page, so that his customers would know that the work had been done "by William Shake-speare."

The same thing happened in the case of the Stationers' Register, which was used by the London publishers to list their forthcoming books and protect their copyrights. Shake-speare's work had been listed in the Stationers' Register since 1593, when *Venus and Adonis* was published, but none of his various publishers had bothered to mention the author's name. Once Shakespeare's name began to appear on title-pages, how-ever, it was only a question of time before it began to be men-tioned in the Stationers' Register, although the names of authors were not usually listed, and an entry of 1600 marks his first appearance: "two books, the one called Much Ado About Nothing, the other the second part of the history of King Henry the Fourth with the humours of Sir John Falstaff. Written by master Shakespeare."

Shakespeare's name grew increasingly important in the world of books as the decade advanced. When *King Lear* was published seven years later Shakespeare's name preceded that of the play on the title-page and the announcement read: "a book called Master William Shakespeare his history of King Lear." In fact, he was so popular with the reading public that a printer got hold of the script of a Globe success written by a different playwright and entered it in the Stationers' Regis-ter as "a book called a Yorkshire Tragedy written by William Shakespeare."

Shakespeare was extremely popular with the general public, whether they bought books or went to the theatre, but he was not considered a very important writer by the literary critics of the period. It is difficult for the average critic to feel that a writer can be really important if he pleases ordinary people, and in any case the Elizabethans were convinced that no play could be a literary success if it broke the rules. Shakespeare had never paid any attention to the classical unities, except in his very early play of *The Comedy of Errors*. He showed murders onstage, and mixed comedy and tragedy together, and in general paid so little attention to what was called "decorum" that it was difficult for any trained critic to take his work seriously.

There was one playwright of the period, a personal friend of Shakespeare's, who worried very much about what he felt to be Shakespeare's careless way of writing. This was Ben Jonson, who had studied all the classical rules and who was determined to bring back pure tragedy and pure comedy to the English stage. Ben Jonson said that Shakespeare lacked "art," by which he meant that Shakespeare refused to follow rules. Even when he wrote a play on a classical subject, like *Julius Caesar*, he refused to treat it in a classical manner, and Jonson objected so strongly to one of the lines in *Julius Caesar* that Shakespeare evidently omitted it to please him. A character in the play had said, "Caesar, thou dost me wrong," and Shakespeare's Caesar had answered, "Caesar did never wrong but with just cause." Jonson said that this remark was "ridiculous," by which he meant that it was not logical. He had forgotten that a dictator is not usually a logical man. Jonson was thinking of Caesar as a character laid out neatly on a piece of paper while Shakespeare was thinking of him as a real human being.

Jonson himself wrote a Roman tragedy, following all the rules, and it was produced at the Globe. It was not a success and the performance is chiefly interesting because Shakespeare acted in it. He and Richard Burbage took the leading roles in the play and their names stand at the head of the cast, with Heminges and Phillips just below. In spite of its failure on the stage, Ben Jonson saw the play into print, and all his literary friends combined to point out to the unobservant public what a masterly work of art he had created. No literary friends combined to do this sort of thing for Shakespeare. His plays were merely issued in cheap popular editions to make money for enterprising publishers like John Danter and Andrew Wise.

Shakespeare was not altogether without honor, of course, in the literary world. The constant appearance of his work in literary anthologies had established him as one of the more prominent of the modern poets, and his name usually occurred on any list of well-known writers of the period. William Camden, for instance, included him on a list of modern poets, and since Camden was one of the greatest scholars of his day his opinion was well worth having. Yet Camden did not single Shakespeare out for any special attention. He merely listed him among the good "wits" of the period, along with Sidney, Spenser and younger writers like Ben Jonson.

Another prominent figure in the world of letters was Gabriel Harvey, who had been a school friend of Sidney's and whom Spenser had praised for his "critic pen." Harvey jotted down some notes on the current literary scene and not only included Shakespeare among the "flourishing" poets of the day but singled his work out for special mention. "The younger sort take much delight in Shakespeare's *Venus and Adonis;* but his *Lucrece,* and his tragedy of *Hamlet, Prince of Denmark,* have it in them to please the wiser sort." Like most literary people, Harvey thought of Shakespeare chiefly in connection with his two narrative poems, and it shows remarkable penetration in a conservative and elderly critic like Harvey

An Introduction to Shakespeare

that he should have been able to recognize *Hamlet* as a work of art. Most people thought of it merely as a popular play-house production at the Globe.

There was some excuse for these people, since a melodrama called *Hamlet* had been in circulation for many years and was a kind of by-word in the theatre business for old-fashioned, exaggerated play-writing. Shakespeare's own company had just produced a play that contained a direct attack on the popular old melodrama with its "whining ghost," and the phrase, "Hamlet, revenge!" was so familiar that it was almost a joke. But Shakespeare never objected to old materials, and he used the shoddy old revenge tragedy as the basis for the most extraordinary play in the English language.

Hamlet is a masterpiece of story-telling, and the bloody, complicated plot is handled with a swiftness and tension that remain unbroken if the play is performed as Shakespeare wrote it. Yet the ultimate power of the play is not due to Shakespeare's skill as a craftsman or even to his almost incredible control over language. It lies in the character of Hamlet, the most remarkable character that any dramatist ever made.

Hamlet was burdened by his own mind. There are few people so fortunate that they have not felt, at one time or another, the weight of the same load, but Hamlet could express in words what most people only vaguely feel. It is not an easy thing to be a human being, and Hamlet carries within himself the confusion and the boredom, the disgust and the fury that nearly every human being has wrestled with in private. "O God! I could be bounded in a nutshell and count myself a king of infinite space, were it not that I have bad dreams."

Hamlet was a prince of great courtesy and much wit, and

he had almost more intelligence than he knew what to do with. He could have done almost anything he wanted, but he did not know what he wanted to do. When his father's ghost told him to commit a murder he could look at the subject from every angle, argue with himself, goad himself and yet know all the time that the traitor was within. A mind of great force and subtlety, turned in on itself in a situation that called for brisk, mindless action, is the tragedy of *Hamlet*, and generation after generation has probed his motives, argued over his inconsistencies and been haunted by its own image in the unhappy prince.

The play was presented by the Chamberlain's company with its usual brilliance. Richard Burbage played Hamlet, and the scene in which he leaps into Ophelia's grave was handled with such effectiveness that one Elizabethan theatregoer never forgot it. There is a legend that Shakespeare played the ghost of Hamlet's father, although whether he played that part or another makes little difference. All the parts were well played, and the fortunate theatregoers at the Globe sent up a roar of approval.

Everyone liked *Hamlet*, and the literary world echoed the public's approval. An author of the period said that every piece of writing ought to be like "friendly Shakespeare's tragedies . . . Faith, it should please all, like Prince Hamlet." The great prince was loved from the first, as he deserved to be, and the Globe theatre had another success by Shakespeare to add to its brilliant and lengthening list.

Chapter 9

HAMLET was published in 1603, the year that the Age of Elizabeth ended. The Queen had not been well when Shakespeare's company went out to her country palace of Richmond to give a play in February, and by the middle of March she was dangerously ill. Every theatre in London was closed, and lamps were hung out to burn all night. Elizabeth lay on cushions, speaking to no one, and on the twenty-fourth of March the lonely, magnificent old woman died.

The Queen was buried in Westminster Abbey and all London watched the four great horses with trappings of black velvet that carried the purple-draped coffin. The Londoners had cause to mourn her, for she had been a very great ruler and had served England well. But no one had more reason to honor her memory than the actors, for she had never ceased to give them her protection and her support.

The new ruler of England was Elizabeth's cousin, James of Scotland, and he was not, in many ways, a very successful king. He was timid and undignified, and he spent far too much money. But James had two things in common with the great monarch who had preceded him: he tried to keep the peace, and he loved plays.

In Scotland James had defended the actors valiantly against the Scottish kirk. In Edinburgh the deacons had tried to suppress the performances of an English actor named Lawrence Fletcher and the King had forced them to cancel their own proclamation. Fletcher was James' favorite actor and as soon as he was crowned King of England he formed a company of players to be known as the King's Men, with Fletcher at the head of the list.

The King's Men were given a royal patent, listing the whole of the company, and the next name after Fletcher was William Shakespeare. The third name was Richard Burbage, and after him came Augustine Phillips, John Heminges, Henry Condell and the rest. The new company was, in fact, merely the Chamberlain's company with Fletcher added. It had become the greatest company in London, and now that the King had taken it under his patronage its position was impregnable for the rest of his reign. The same thing was true of the two lesser companies, which were put under the protection of Prince Henry and Queen Anne. The mayor of London disliked the players as much as ever but there was nothing he could do to harm them.

King James did not stay in London after his coronation, for the plague had driven everyone out of town. So he asked his company of actors to give a play for him at Wilton House, where he was staying as the guest of one of his noblemen. Wilton House was the residence of the Earl of Pembroke, who later became a good friend to the whole of the company and especially to Richard Burbage. When Heminges and Condell, many years later, brought together the first collected edition of Shakespeare's plays, it was to the Earl of Pembroke and his brother that they dedicated it.

When Shakespeare's company played at Wilton House that December, two of the men who had taken shares in the Globe were no longer with them. One of the missing members was Will Kempe, who had left them shortly after the theatre was built and turned his share in it back to his fellow actors. His place had been taken by Robert Armin, who was a playwright as well as a comedian and who probably acted most of Shakespeare's later clowns.

Another missing actor was Thomas Pope, who had evidently retired because of ill health. He made his will in Southwark the previous July, carefully remembering all the fatherless children in his household down to the eleven-months-old baby who was the latest addition; and he died the following February. Another of the original shareholders of the Globe, Augustine Phillips, died a year later at his country estate, remembering all his fellow actors in his will. Burbage and Heminges were left silver bowls and Shakespeare was left a gold piece. Phillips also remembered the boy who had been brought up in his household as an acting apprentice. "I give to Samuel Gilbourne, my late apprentice, the sum of forty shillings, and my mouse-colored velvet hose and a white taffety doublet, a black taffety suit, my purple cloak, sword and dagger and my bass viol."

Only three men were now left of the original group of "deserving men" who had put up the Globe theatre. They were William Shakespeare, Richard Burbage and John Heminges, now the senior members of the most important acting company in England.

The prosperity they had known in the reign of Elizabeth continued in the reign of James. Nothing was changed except that the new monarch was in such a hurry to see plays that the Christmas season at Court was started the first of November instead of the old date of December 26. The King's Men put on most of the productions, and most of the plays they used had been written by William Shakespeare.

The official who made up the 1604 expense account for the Office of the Revels arranged his report neatly in three columns, the first for the name of the company, the second for the name of the play and the third for the name of "the poet which made the play." Seven of Shakespeare's plays appear on the careful list, and five of them were old ones. The King's Men presented *The Comedy of Errors, Love's Labour's Lost, The Merry Wives of Windsor, Henry V* and *The Merchant of Venice,* and the last of these pleased King James so much when it was presented on Shrove Sunday that he "again commanded" it to be played two days later.

The King's Men also presented two other plays of Shakespeare's. They opened the season on the first of November with *Othello,* which was presented before King James in the banqueting hall with Richard Burbage in the title role, and on St. Stephen's Night in the great hall they gave *Measure for Measure.*

Shakespeare took the plots of both these plays from a book of Italian short stories by Giraldi Cinthio, and in the case of *Measure for Measure* he found himself in constant difficulties with the plot. He put real people into a complicated, old-fashioned story, making it partly a comedy, with its disguises and its happy ending, and partly a tragedy, with its bitter, mocking atmosphere of a decaying Vienna. Some of the writing is Shakespeare at his best, but the plot seems formless and confusing to a modern reader who cannot accept, as an Elizabethan audience could, the arbitrary conventions of a folk story set against a realistic background.

In the case of *Othello,* on the other hand, Shakespeare was completely successful with what seems to be, at first glance, an even more unpromising plot. For Cinthio tells an unconvincing and bloody story of a Moorish soldier who is told by one of his officers that his wife is unfaithful. He and the officer kill her with a sandbag and the state punishes them for the crime.

Shakespeare transforms the story, and makes it real. Othello, the Moorish soldier, is already afraid that his wife cannot really be in love with him, for he is older than she is and of a different color. Once Iago implants the idea of his wife's unfaithfulness in Othello's mind, his jealousy begins feeding on itself until it is out of control and, loving his wife, he kills her. As for Iago, he is so courteous in his behavior and apparently so anxious to believe the best of his captain's wife that there is no reason whatever for Othello to suspect him. Nor can Desdemona herself stop the tragedy, for she has been brought up as a "super-subtle Venetian" and cannot understand the violence of her Moorish husband. An ordinary woman would have realized that he was growing insanely jealous, but Desdemona merely thought he was troubled by political problems, since she knew that he loved her and that she had done nothing wrong. Shakespeare was well aware of the terrible force of an emotion that gets out of control, and he saw in Cinthio's trivial little melodrama the shadow of the monstrous growth that he built up into the tragic violence of *Othello*.

Another of Shakespeare's great tragedies was also taken from an unpromising story. Macbeth was an early Scottish king whose career was recorded in Holinshed's *Chronicles*, the popular history book from which Shakespeare took so many of his stories. Holinshed reports that Macbeth was a "valiant gentleman" who had an ambitious wife and too much faith in witches. He committed several murders, but on the whole he was a satisfactory king and reigned seventeen years.

Shakespeare turned this commonplace material into a swift and terrifying tragedy, with the very minds of the people soaked in blood. If *Othello* is a tragedy of jealousy, *Macbeth* is a tragedy of ambition, and in each case a natural emotion gets completely out of control and destroys the people who have harbored it.

Macbeth and his wife thought they could murder the king of Scotland and then with quiet minds take possession of the crown. Lady Macbeth looked at their bloody hands and believed it was an easy thing to forget a murder. "A little water clears us of this deed." She did not realize the existence of what Macbeth was to call the torture of the mind, or the fact they would be forced into further murders to make themselves safe. Nor were they safe then, after all their murders. As Macbeth said,

> the times have been
> That, when the brains were out, the man would die . . .

but Macbeth's victims remain alive in his mind. Lady Macbeth keeps a light burning continuously in her room because she can no longer endure the dark, and the blood on her hands that a little water would once wash off is now there continually in her dreams. No matter how often she rubs her hands she cannot get them clean.

Shakespeare was now lord of language and could say anything he wished, and he used every image of darkness and blood and disorder to bring to the audience the terror of committing murder and the helplessness of a mind that had driven itself into its own pit. Macbeth had already died before Macduff finally killed him because the act of living had lost all meaning for him:

> it is a tale
> Told by an idiot, full of sound and fury,
> Signifying nothing.

For his third great tragedy of this period, *Antony and Cleopatra*, Shakespeare turned to Plutarch's *Lives*. This was a nobler source than Cinthio or Holinshed, and as a result Shakespeare was able to use much more of the original material. For instance, the description of Cleopatra in her barge is taken direct from Plutarch's account, except that Plutarch's prose has been turned into the most golden of poetry.

> The barge she sat in, like a burnished throne,
> Burned on the water; the poop was beaten gold,
> Purple the sails, and so perfumed that
> The winds were love-sick with them . . .

Shakespeare was doing a difficult thing in *Antony and Cleopatra*, for he was telling the story of two middle-aged lovers who destroyed themselves for love. It is easy to get sympathy for young lovers like Romeo and Juliet, but Cleopatra was in her late thirties and Antony over fifty. Even Plutarch disapproved of Antony, whose passion for Cleopatra he calls the "last and extremest mischief of all."

Shakespeare does not disapprove of Antony, and he does not judge him. He merely presents him, a great man and great soldier who is wrecking himself for love as Othello did for jealousy and Macbeth for ambition. As for Cleopatra, she is

An Introduction to Shakespeare

Shakespeare's most intricate human being since Hamlet and his most outrageous since Falstaff. She is a wanton and a coward, unreasonable and jealous and violent. She is also a great queen and the most enchanting woman he ever made. "A man could not possibly but be taken," remarks Plutarch regretfully, and Shakespeare makes that statement true.

The background of *Antony and Cleopatra* is the whole of the civilized world—Alexandria, Rome, Messina, the plains of Syria, Pompey's galley, Athens and Egypt. Only on a stage like the Globe's, with its lack of rigid settings and its complete flexibility, could a play of such rapid movement be presented. There was almost nothing that could not be done with such a stage, and almost nothing that its greatest playwright did not undertake. Shakespeare had an art that was almost without limits, and as a writer he is as much a "wonderful piece of work" as his own Cleopatra.

The other great tragedy that Shakespeare gave the Globe was *King Lear*. Lear was a legendary British king and the Londoners had read about him in Holinshed's *Chronicles*. There was also a play on Lear in existence, a rather dull, wooden play with a happy ending, and what Shakespeare saw in this to use it as the basis of his own tragedy it is hard to say. He makes additions that only confuse the once-tidy plot and he adds scenes of violence that have no real motivation. It is as though a storm had swept through the old story, dislocating it into a mirror of the madness that seizes Lear. Shakespeare never wrote more remarkable poetry or produced a more frightening play. Its subject is old age and poverty and insanity, and the prosperous playwright at the Globe forced his equally prosperous audience to enter into a broken and agonized world and then exalted it through his poetry.

An Introduction to Shakespeare

The part of Lear is a formidable one for an actor, but Shakespeare had Richard Burbage. The two men had grown up in the theatre together, from the youthful melodrama of *Richard III* to the subtlety of *Hamlet* and the passion of *Othello*, and Burbage had developed his capacity to play Lear after a dozen years of daily association with Shakespeare himself. He could rise to the violence of Lear's defiance of the storm on the heath, and he could drop his voice to the drained, childlike weariness of the final scene:

> I am a very foolish, fond old man,
> Fourscore and upward, not an hour more or less;
> And, to deal plainly,
> I fear I am not in my perfect mind . . .

Most of the plays that Shakespeare wrote in the reign of King James did not get into print. The company no longer needed money, as it evidently had around 1600, and it kept a stern eye on the scripts of its leading dramatist. A publisher named Nathaniel Butter succeeded in getting hold of a faulty copy of *King Lear* in 1608, and many years later a publisher printed *Othello* with the remark that the author's name on the title-page was all that was needed to sell the book. But most of the plays remained in manuscript, safely stored away by the King's Men, and if a Londoner wanted to enjoy any of Shakespeare's later plays he had to join the thousands each week who paid their pennies into the waiting hands of the gatherers at the Globe.

Chapter 10

ACHANGE was coming over the theatre-going public during these years in which Shakespeare was writing his plays. More and more people were beginning to feel that it was wrong to go to plays and that acting companies should not be tolerated in a well-governed community.

Many small groups of people had been feeling this way for some time. The mayor and aldermen of London had opposed the actors from the first, and both Oxford and Cambridge refused to permit their students to attend professional shows although they were free to do amateur acting. But the most determined enemies of the theatre were a group called the Puritans.

The Puritans had a very austere kind of religion and they condemned every form of amusement, from dancing to card-playing. But they singled out the stage as a special invention of the devil, and when Shakespeare was in his twenties there were already pamphlets that described the theatres as sinks of "pride and prodigality, villainy and blasphemy" and called the actors everything from vipers to hell-hounds.

At first the Puritans were a very small group and the actors hardly noticed them except to make fun of them on the stage. The actor who played Falstaff, for instance, would parody the uplifted eyes and sing-song voice of the Puritans when he remarked virtuously to Prince Hal: "Thou hast done much harm upon me, Hal; God forgive thee for it! Before I knew thee, Hal, I knew nothing; and now am I, if a man should speak truly, little better than one of the wicked." The Puritans divided mankind into the wicked and the saved, and one sure way to get into the former classification was to go to plays.

A huge port city like London, with its varied, lively, cosmopolitan population, could absorb a great many Puritans without their having a direct effect on the theatre, but in a small town like Stratford they could make their influence felt. There had been Puritan families in Stratford since Shakespeare was a boy. The Barnhursts were one and the Hathaways another, and it may be that the reason Shakespeare's wife, Anne Hathaway, did not make a home for him in London was that she was a Puritan like her brother Bartholomew. Three years after the Globe was built, the Stratford Puritans had become numerous enough to get the local Council to pass a decree forbidding any more plays in town. If anyone gave a license to the actors he was to be fined ten shillings, and a decade later this fine was raised to the large sum of ten pounds.

Even in London the actors found that there was a narrowing down of the easy-going, middle-class audience that had been the mainstay of the public theatres in Elizabeth's day, and some of the newer theatre companies made a direct bid for the patronage of smaller, more sophisticated audiences who could afford large admission prices. Plays were presented in roofed-in, lighted theatres that were called "private" theatres, and there was an emphasis on good music and clever scripts. Many playwrights who had not been able to write successfully for the great public amphitheatres turned with

relief to the more intellectual atmosphere of the private theatres, where the parts were all acted by boys and everything
was on a smaller and neater scale. Nearly every dramatist in
London worked at one time or another for the boy actors, and
the only two notable exceptions were Thomas Heywood,
chief playwright of the Queen's Men, and William Shakespeare, chief playwright of the King's.

Nevertheless, a private theatre had many advantages, since
it was not easy to persuade the Londoners to cross a cold grey
river like the Thames on a winter afternoon to shiver in an
unroofed theatre like the Globe. Richard Burbage's father had
made the experiment of building a roofed-in theatre on the
London side of the Thames just before he died; but he put it
up in an aristocratic section called the Blackfriars and the residents protested so vigorously that he was not allowed to open
it. Richard Burbage inherited the building and rented it out
to one of the boys' companies. The Blackfriars residents did
not object to this, since the tradition of boy actors stretched
back respectably to the boys' choir of the Chapel Royal. It
was the adult actors to whom they objected, since it was felt
that they brought rowdy customers with them.

The boys' acting company at the Blackfriars got into trouble
with the government over its choice of plays and in 1608 it
was dissolved. This left the theatre empty, and it occurred to
Richard Burbage that there was no need to encourage rivals.
The King's Men could use the Blackfriars theatre themselves
and save their customers a long, cold trip over the river in
winter weather. There was no precedent for adult actors appearing in a roofed-in private theatre, but the Burbages were
never afraid of trying something new.

Richard and Cuthbert financed the Blackfriars theatre in

the same way they had financed the Globe. They asked some of the leading actors of the company to come in with them on shares. The two most prominent members of the new syndicate were of course William Shakespeare and John Heminges. Heminges' close friend, Henry Condell, was also invited to join the Blackfriars syndicate and so was Will Sly, another old friend who had known both Burbage and Heminges for the past twenty years and who was a neighbor of the Burbages in St. Leonard's parish.

The actors managed the Blackfriars theatre in the same intelligent and harmonious way they managed the Globe, and the new venture was a success from the first. The residents of the Blackfriars found that their worst suspicions were confirmed and they sent a petition to the government protesting that "there was daily such a resort of people and such a multitude of coaches (many of them hackney coaches bringing people of all sorts) that at times the streets could not contain them."

The King's Men now had two theatres, and Shakespeare's last plays were probably given in both. Two of these plays, *The Winter's Tale* and *Cymbeline*, show Shakespeare's attitude towards plots at its most casual, for he picked up the first from an old-fashioned story of Robert Greene's and *Cymbeline* was a mixture of Holinshed and an Italian melodrama. Sometimes Shakespeare could take an unreasonable situation and make the characters in it so convincing that the situation becomes convincing also. But his imagination did not catch fire from either of the two plots and they seem more like fairy tales than the actions of human beings. Imogen, the heroine of *Cymbeline*, would be a very real person if she could have been given a chance, but the plot overwhelms her; and the delightful Autolycus is a wanderer around the edges of the story in *The Winter's Tale* rather than an essential part of it.

What makes the two plays so loved is the poetry in which they are written. They have a springtime loveliness that matches Perdita's flowers,

> . . . daffodils
> That come before the swallow dares, and take
> The winds of March with beauty . . .

There is disaster in both plays, and *Cymbeline* is listed as a tragedy; yet even death is made beautiful in the wonderful lament that begins, "Fear no more the heat o' the sun," and the same play contains the prettiest morning song in the English language.

> Hark! hark! the lark at heaven's gate sings,
>   And Phoebus 'gins arise,
> His steeds to water at those springs
>   On chaliced flowers that lies;
> And winking Mary-buds begin
>   To ope their golden eyes:
> With everything that pretty is,
>   My lady sweet, arise:
>   Arise, arise!

In that age of great singing voices, Shakespeare's was the greatest. And even at the close of his career, with its weight of experience and knowledge of evil, he could still write like a young poet who had never known anything but spring.

The third play of the series is *The Tempest*, which is probably the last play Shakespeare wrote before he retired from the acting profession. *The Tempest* is frankly a fairy tale, full of enchantments and spirits and a monster, and it was so intricate to stage that the Globe must have been crowded with the pulleys and extra machinery that were needed to show Prospero's magic onstage. Yet in a way it is the simplest of all Shakespeare's plays, for the action takes place on a single island in a single afternoon. It has the tight, brilliant construction that Shakespeare usually reserved for his tragedies rather than his comedies, and there is an unearthly magic about the poetry itself that outdistances even Prospero's spells.

A decade earlier one of Shakespeare's characters had said of plays: "The best in this kind are but shadows." To Prospero the world itself is a shadow and no more real than a play.

> Our revels now are ended. These our actors,
> As I foretold you, were all spirits and
> Are melted into air, into thin air:
> And, like the baseless fabric of this vision,
> The cloud-capped towers, the gorgeous palaces,
> The solemn temples, the great globe itself,
> Yea, all which it inherit, shall dissolve
> And, like this insubstantial pageant faded,
> Leave not a rack behind. We are such stuff
> As dreams are made on, and our little life
> Is rounded with a sleep.

A more self-conscious dramatist might have made this Prospero's final speech; but Shakespeare drops it casually into the play and Prospero's final speech is actually a request for the applause of the audience. Shakespeare, unlike some of his later admirers, did not think of his plays as repositories of wisdom and poetry. He thought of them as plays, and both the wisdom and the poetry were merely his lavish extra gift to the fortunate audiences of London.

An Introduction to Shakespeare

The Tempest was produced at Court in the Christmas season of 1611, and it was shortly before this that Shakespeare retired from his acting career. He went back to Stratford and settled down there in the large house he had bought many years earlier. New Place was a handsome and comfortable residence, with its large garden and its ten fireplaces, and it had a brick wall to separate it from the busy street outside. Shakespeare was one of the most prominent landowners in the district, since he had also bought a great deal of farm land around Stratford, and John Shakespeare's dream of establishing the family among the landed gentry of Warwickshire had finally been made a reality by his actor son.

Shakespeare kept up his associations with London, and he was in town frequently on business. A year or so after he retired he bought a house and yard near the Blackfriars theatre as an investment, so that he was a London landowner as well as a Stratford one. On another occasion he joined Richard Burbage in designing a shield for a nobleman to carry at a royal tournament. Shakespeare wrote the motto that was to go on it while Burbage, who was a portrait painter as well as an actor, did the accompanying picture.

Shakespeare also was called to London to testify in a lawsuit. At about the time King James came to the throne, Shakespeare had moved from Southwark to become the lodger of a family on the west side of town. The family consisted of Mr. and Mrs. Mountjoy and their only daughter Mary, and Shakespeare had helped Mrs. Mountjoy arrange a marriage between Mary and a young apprentice who was being trained in the family business. Christopher Mountjoy quarreled steadily with his new son-in-law, and the case finally went to court.

Shakespeare testified on the side of the young people and they won the case.

Shakespeare also wrote a play for the King's Men after his retirement—the history play of *Henry VIII*. A new play by William Shakespeare was an event, and the company spared no expense in putting it on. Costumes were designed that were correct to the last detail, the guards in their embroidered coats, the knights with special replicas of the Order of the Garter, and all the coronets and sceptres accurately and gorgeously portrayed; and special strips of matting were ordered to protect the actors' expensive costumes from the floor of the stage.

The first act of *Henry VIII* calls for the King's entrance during a dance, and to make this especially effective the company decided to fire off a cannon from the roof. Cannons had been used in this way for years and nothing had happened, in spite of the obvious danger from fire, but on this particular June day the Globe was unlucky. A little burning paper fell on the thatched roof and no one noticed it because everyone was "attentive to the show." It smouldered and then broke into flame, and within less than two hours the Globe theatre had burned to the ground.

No one was hurt, and the company decided at once to rebuild. John Heminges handled the financial details, and since Shakespeare was still a shareholder he probably contributed to the costs. Within a year the theatre was "new builded in a far fairer manner than before" and the King's Men continued on their prosperous career.

But Shakespeare gave them no more plays. On the 23rd of April, 1616, he died in Stratford and was buried in the local church. He was given a special position of honor inside the chancel rail, but this was not because he was a great writer; it was because he had bought some of the church tithes and was therefore a lay rector.

Shakespeare left a careful will behind him, itemizing even his wearing apparel and his bowl of gilded silver. His only son had died nearly twenty years earlier and there was no one to carry on the family name, but he left his house and lands to his elder daughter in the hope that she would some day have a son. His will does not mention his plays, since they did not belong to him but to his company. But it does mention his "fellows John Heminges, Richard Burbage and Henry Condell." These were the only surviving members of the original group that had worked together since the days of Queen Elizabeth, and Shakespeare left them each money to buy a memorial ring to wear in his memory.

Chapter 11

Heminges and Condell did not need memorial rings to remind them of their friend. They had worked with him for nearly twenty years in a close and affectionate companionship and his plays were still a living part of the company's repertoire. Richard Burbage had died three years after Shakespeare, and new performers took the parts the original company of actors had played; but the plays themselves went on being loved and applauded. As a friend of Heminges and Condell put it:

> . . . let but Falstaff come,
> Hal, Poins, the rest—you scarce shall have a room
> All is so pestered; let but Beatrice
> And Benedick be seen, lo, in a trice
> The cockpit, galleries, boxes, all are full . . .

Twenty different publishers had by this time made money out of Shakespeare's plays. They had presented them to the public in cheap quarto editions, all on poor paper and many with inaccurate texts. They had not been able to get hold of the scripts of some of Shakespeare's greatest plays, like *Macbeth* and *The Tempest*, and so they had been using his name on the title-page to sell plays like *The London Prodigal* that he had never written.

An Introduction to Shakespeare

Heminges and Condell knew that Shakespeare's plays might be lost altogether as the cheap quartos wore out and the last of the original acting company died, and so they conceived the idea of having all the plays printed in a single book. They did not do this to get money or credit for themselves. "We have but collected them, and done an office to the dead, to procure his orphans guardians; without ambition either of self-profit or fame; only to keep the memory of so worthy a friend and fellow alive as was our Shakespeare." Heminges and Condell knew something about orphans, for two actors in the company left fatherless children to their charge. In Shakespeare's case, his real offspring were not his two daughters in Stratford; they were the children of his mind, his thirty-six plays.

Heminges and Condell had undertaken a difficult task in collecting the plays and arranging for their publication, and they remarked feelingly, "Do not envy his friends the office of their care and pain, to have collected and published them." Editing the plays was difficult enough, since the company scripts seem to have been in a haphazard state and in some cases the best solution was to use a late printed edition rather than a playhouse copy.

The publishing was still more difficult since there were too many plays to be published cheaply in quarto. The volume would have been so thick as to be unmanageable. The only solution was to put them out in a tall folio volume, and plays were not printed in folio. Big, handsome books of this kind were reserved for science and theology and other important subjects. It was true that Ben Jonson had issued some of his plays in folio, but he had also included poems and masques, and in any case Jonson was a prominent man who had been given honorary degrees by both universities. There might be buyers among the well-to-do for Jonson's elegant productions but not for the work of a common playwright like Shakespeare.

Nevertheless, Heminges and Condell were convinced that their "friend and fellow" was worthy of a folio edition. They seem to have had trouble getting a printer and finally settled on William Jaggard, who had printed an earlier collection of Shakespeare's plays that Heminges and Condell had rightly denounced as a fraud. Yet he was apparently the best they could get, and Jaggard in his turn economized where he could. He bought cheap paper and spent less money than he should on proof-reading, and there were no illustrations except a plain engraved head of Shakespeare as a frontispiece. The volume was planned for publication in 1622 but there was a delay, probably caused by lack of money, and it finally came out the following year.

A book of this kind was usually advertised by commendatory verses in the front of it, supplied by the author's literary friends. Ben Jonson's folio had nine poems in it, all from prominent people, but Shakespeare's had only four. The first two of these refer gracefully to Shakespeare's career as an actor, the third prophesies that the book will outlast the marble monument that had just been put up at Stratford, and the fourth was written by the great Ben Jonson himself.

Jonson's contribution was an act of friendship, for he knew Heminges and Condell well. He had written six plays for the company, and Heminges and Condell had appeared in them all. Moreover, Jonson had been a close personal friend of Shakespeare himself. "I loved the man and do honor his memory . . . He was, indeed, honest, and of an open and free nature." Jonson did not always approve of Shakespeare's way of writing but he loved him dearly, and Shakespeare was one of the few literary men with whom Jonson never had a quarrel.

Jonson wrote eighty lines, prefaced by the title: "To the memory of my beloved, the author, Master William Shakespeare and what he hath left us," and he voiced for the first time the kind of praise that no one in Shakespeare's lifetime had had the wit to give him. Jonson was an ardent classicist, which Shakespeare certainly was not, and yet when Jonson made a list of the mighty Greeks he put Shakespeare beside them.

He was not of an age, but for all time.

It was just as well that all Shakespeare's plays had been gathered together safely in print, since nineteen years after the publication of the folio the Puritans closed every theatre in England. The King's Men were dissolved as an organization, never to form again, and the Globe theatre ceased to exist.

Thanks to Heminges and Condell, Shakespeare's plays were still available to the public; and they read them with the same enthusiasm with which they had once gone to the Globe to see them acted. The young men at Oxford studied *Romeo and Juliet* so ardently that the page which contains the balcony scene still shows the mark of their devoted elbows; and when young Margaret Cavendish and a friend played the game of confessing whom they loved best, Margaret found there was no Englishman she held in her heart except "our countryman Shakespeare."

There were no professional actors left in England, but there were still amateurs who saw to it that Shakespeare's plays were kept alive on the stage after a fashion. Part of *A Midsummer Night's Dream* was issued as "the merry conceited humours of Bottom the weaver, as it hath been often publicly acted by some of His Majesty's Comedians, and lately, privately, presented by several apprentices for their harmless recreation, with great applause." If the faithful apprentices could not go to see Shakespeare's plays acted, they could act them out themselves; and Puck and Falstaff at least were kept alive on the stage during the period of the Puritan Commonwealth.

A king returned to the throne of England in 1660 and he brought the theatre back with him. But King Charles had been living in France, and it was the elegant French theatre he brought. As John Evelyn noted in his diary the following year: "I saw *Hamlet, Prince of Denmark*, played, but now the old plays begin to disgust this refined age, since His Majesty's being so long abroad." Shakespeare's plays returned to the stage again, but they were toned down and rewritten in order to please a Court audience in silks and periwigs.

Throughout the whole of the seventeenth century, Shakespeare had been thought of as a popular writer and had not been taken very seriously by the critics. Neither Bolton nor Peacham, writing shortly after his death, had included him in their lists of English writers. As a playwright he was usually not ranked much higher than John Fletcher, although it was agreed that he had "a certain wild and native elegance" of his own.

A very prominent critic at the end of the seventeenth century said sternly that Shakespeare had a barbarous disregard for the rules of play-writing and had worked much too hard to please his audience of "carpenters and cobblers." He was willing to admit that Shakespeare was fairly good at comedy, but "in tragedy he appears quite out of his element; his brains are turned, he raves and rambles, without any coherence, any spark of reason, or any rules to control him." Even John Dryden, the first really powerful voice raised after Ben Jonson's in Shakespeare's defense, admitted that he had committed "some errors not to be avoided in that age." But Dryden insisted that in spite of his defects he was a remarkable writer and a great poet. "When he describes anything, you more than see it, you feel it too."

The average reader of the period agreed with Dryden. He might not have Dryden's learning, but he knew what he liked, and he greeted Shakespeare's characters as friends and contemporaries. The first illustrated edition of the plays came out in 1709, with Hamlet in a periwig and Macbeth in an embroidered waistcoat, and was enthusiastically received. The edition was not quite as stylish as it looked, since the elaborate frontispiece portrait of Shakespeare surrounded by allegorical ladies was actually a cheap copy of a French engraving that had already been used for the plays of Corneille. But Shakespeare's readers were not looking for elegance; they were looking for delight, and the six fat little volumes gave it to them.

All through the eighteenth century the illustrated editions continued. It was the Age of Reason, the age of silks and elegance, and the illustrators did all they could to tame Shakespeare. Macbeth saw the ghost of Banquo in a stylish dining room heavy with fashionable draperies, and Othello murdered Desdemona in a charming Georgian interior. Shakespeare's own portrait became increasingly involved with allegory, and one edition even had an instructive frontispiece labelled "Shakespeare holding up the Mirror to Dignified Guilt." Prominent literary men like Alexander Pope and Dr. Samuel Johnson edited the plays, and although there was still some unfavorable criticism it was generally agreed that Shakespeare had been a great, if faulty, poet.

Early in the nineteenth century there was a revolt against the classical theories that had been believed since Shakespeare's boyhood, and as soon as this happened Shakespeare could at last be officially approved by the critics. The rules had changed and Shakespeare was no longer a slightly barbarous giant. Instead he had become godlike and could do no wrong. His plays were now bound in handsome presentation volumes and the nobler bits were forcibly assigned to be memorized. Even this, which in any other writer would have meant a slow turning into memorial marble, did not injure Shakespeare. People still read him for pleasure, and they memorized the songs and speeches for their own enjoyment and not because they had become required reading.

The wave of idolatry went on rising throughout the nineteenth century. Shakespeare's birthplace in Stratford became a shrine and he was reverently called the "Bard of Avon." This was not a particularly suitable title for a practicing London playwright who saw the Avon only on occasional trips to the country, but by this time all his theatrical connections —and especially the fact he had been an actor—were being ignored as being too low-class for a Bard. Thousands of books poured from the presses about him, and then other thousands pointing out how wrong the previous ones had been. Shakespear's characters were brooded over and analyzed and argued about, and the question whether Hamlet was mad or only pretending to be used up more paper than Heminges and Condell had required for the First Folio. The United States became as excited over the subject as England, and every year the books and articles multiplied.

Nor did Shakespeare confine himself to the English-speaking world. The first foreign country to welcome him was Germany, for English actors were popular in Germany even during Shakespeare's lifetime and it was natural that his plays should be a part of their repertoire. Three years after Heminges and Condell published the First Folio, an English acting company went to Dresden and presented versions of *Hamlet*, *The Merchant of Venice*, *Romeo and Juliet* and *Julius Caesar*. *Hamlet* in particular appealed so powerfully to the German temperament that by the end of the eighteenth century six different actors were interpreting Hamlet on the German stage and in the next hundred years twenty different translations were made of the play. The cult also spilled over into neighboring Hungary, and the Viennese were attending Shakespeare's plays at the time of the American Revolution.

France and Italy took somewhat longer to welcome Shakespeare. The theory of classical rules for playwrights had been started by French and Italian critics, and since Shakespeare ignored the rules, they in turn ignored him. Voltaire was the first prominent literary figure in France to draw attention to Shakespeare, and while Voltaire admitted he had genius he nevertheless denounced him as a barbarian who possessed neither good manners nor good sense. Throughout the Age of Reason, Voltaire's opinion was more or less law in western Europe, but when the Romantic Revival came to Italy in the nineteenth century, Shakespeare came with it. The Italians were at first confused by his irregularities and when *Othello* was first produced in Milan it was hooted off the stage. Eleven years later it was tried again in the same theatre and was a complete success.

It is difficult to translate poetry successfully, and yet all over the world Shakespeare's plays began to appear in translations. *Romeo and Juliet* turned up in Arabic and Danish, *Othello* in Hebrew and Portuguese, and *Hamlet* became a citizen of the whole world. There were editions of *Hamlet* in everything from Slovak to Swedish and one gallant translator even put the play into Esperanto. The great prince was Hamleti to the Albanians, Amleto to the Italians, and Ἁμλετ to the Greeks, and in each country he made himself altogether at home.

Shakespeare's plays were also welcomed in Asia and settled down there as though they were natives. The Japanese actors made Othello the Governor-general of Formosa, with Bianca a geisha-girl and Roderigo a bank president. In India, on the other hand, Othello became a dark-skinned adventurer from the south and Desdemona a high-class Hindu lady. A Bombay audience applauded the sleep-walking scene in *Macbeth* so violently that the play had to be temporarily halted, and all over India the galleries cheered Isabella in *Measure for Measure* and flocked to see Ganapatrao play Hamlet.

An Elizabethan playwright had conquered the world, and no one would have been more startled by the achievement than Shakespeare's own contemporaries. They had thought of him as a popular local playwright, and they had never dreamed each succeeding generation would see its own image in his great art and believe that he wrote for them alone. Even Ben Jonson, who said that Shakespeare was "not of an age but for all time," could not have realized that he was speaking the literal truth.

Among all Shakespeare's contemporaries, it was John

An Introduction to Shakespeare

Heminges and Henry Condell who had the greatest faith in the future. They were convinced that the reputation of their "friend and fellow" would be safe if only his work could be made available to the ordinary reading public.

. . . It is not our province, who only gather his works and give them to you, to praise him. It is yours that read him . . . Read him, therefore; and again and again; and if then you do not like him, surely you are in manifest danger not to understand him. And so we leave him to other of his friends, whom, if you need, can be your guides; if you need them not, you can lead yourselves and others. And such readers we wish him.

John Heminges
Henry Condell

Their wish was answered. It was such readers he got, and no other writer in the world's history has been loved by so many people or has given so much happiness.

INDEX

Index

117

Index

Index

Ford, Mrs., 75
Formosa, 113
France, 72, 112

Ganapatrao, 113
Germany, 27, 112
Gilbourne, Samuel, 87
Globe theatre, 69-71, 77, 81, 84, 87, 92, 93, 97, 98, 100, 102, 108
Gloucester, 14
Gorboduc, 21
Greeks, the, 13, 113
Greene, Robert, 22-24, 25, 28, 31, 98

Hal, Prince, *see* Henry V
Hamlet, see Shakespeare, plays
Hamlet, 36, 83-84, 92, 110, 111, 112, 113
Haphazard, 14
Harrison, John, 34, 35
Harvey, Gabriel, 82-83
Hathaway, Anne, 25, 96
Hathaway, Bartholomew, 96
Hathaway family, 25, 96
Hebrew, 113
Heminges, John, 36-37, 55, 56, 57, 61, 69, 82, 86, 87, 98, 102, 103, 105; as editor of the First Folio, 37, 86, 106-108, 111, 114
Heminges, Rebecca, 56-57
Henry IV, see Shakespeare, plays
Henry IV, 43
Henry V, see Shakespeare, plays

Henry V (Prince Hal), 43, 45, 71, 96, 105
Henry VI, see Shakespeare, plays
Henry VIII, see Shakespeare, plays
Henry, Prince, 86
Heywood, Thomas, 28, 97
Holinshed's *Chronicles*, 29, 89-90, 91, 92, 98
Horestes, 13
Hotspur, 44-45
Hungary, 112
Hymen, 73

Iago, 89
Imogen, 98
Inclination, 14
India, 113
inns, 17, 18, 38
Ireland, 71
Iris, 60
Isabella, 113
Italian theatre, 30, 46, 57, 59
Italy, 57, 112-113

Jaggard, William, 107
James, King, 85-86, 87, 88
Japan, 113
Jew of Malta, The, see Marlowe, Christopher
Jews, the, 48-49, 72
Joan of Arc, 28, 29
John, King, 41, 58
Johnson, Dr. Samuel, 110-111
Jonah, 23

Index

Index

Index

Index

498

$\dfrac{12}{6}$

8.44

Level 5

$D\dfrac{3}{4}$ $Ed.4$